I was a necklace Hanging decorate your lips Closer closer closer to you Closer got

was a velvet bed Draped down your front When you feel the time was right I'd

you Closer closer closer to round your back Right next to your skin Tryin' to make

up Closer closer closer to you If I had my wishes If I had my way I'd be all the

in you walking by Closer Wish I was a cushion Clinging to your shape Every

wouldn't have to beg I'd be closer closer to you Closer got to get closer closer to you

around that I was a hat I wrapped just hanging round your leg When I am dream

I was a necklace Hanging decorate your lips Closer closer closer to you Closer got

Twelfth Night

莎翁戏剧经典

第十二夜

〔英〕威廉·莎士比亚 著
支荩忠 注释

商务印书馆
SINCE 1897 The Commercial Press
2016年·北京

威廉·莎士比亚

图 1

图 2（见 4 页）

—*An apartment in the* DUKE*'s palace.*

Enter DUKE, CURIO, *and other* LORDS; MUSICIANS *attending.*

DUKE. If music be the food of love, play on;
Give me excess of it, that, surfeiting,
The appetite may sicken, and so die.

图 3（见 10 页）

—OLIVIA'S *house*.

Enter SIR TOBY BELCH *and* MARIA.

SIR TOBY. What a plague means my niece, to take the death of her brother thus? I am sure care's an enemy to life.

MARIA. By my troth, Sir Toby, you must come in earlier o'nights: your cousin, my lady, takes great exceptions to your ill hours.

图 **4**（见 14 页）

Enter SIR ANDREW AGUECHEEK.

SIR ANDREW.Sir Toby Belch! how now,Sir Toby Belch!

图 5（见 14 页）

MARIA. Now, sir, 'thought is free': I pray you, bring your hand to the buttery-bar and let it drink.

SIR ANDREW. Wherefore, sweetheart? What's your metaphor?

图 6（见 40 页）

OLIVIA. I do I know not what, and fear to find
Mine eye too great a flatterer for my mind.
Fate, show thy force: ourselves we do not owe;
What is decreed must be, and be this so.

图 7（见 42 页）

— *The sea-coast*.

Enter ANTONIO *and* SEBASTIAN.

ANTONIO. Will you stay no longer? nor will you not that I go with you?

SEBASTIAN. By your patience, no.

图 8（见 54 页）

CLOWN. Yes, by Saint Anne, and ginger shall be hot i' the mouth too.

SIR TOBY. Thou'rt i' the right. Go, sir, rub your chain with crums. A stoup of wine, Maria!

MALVOLIO. Mistress Mary, if you prized my lady's favor at any thing more than contempt, you would not give means for this uncivil rule: she shall know of it, by this hand.

图 9（见 68 页）

MARIA. Get ye all three into the box-tree: Malvolio's coming down this walk: he has been yonder i'the sun practicing behavior to his own shadow this half hour.

图 10（见 78 页）

SIR TOBY. I could marry this wench for this device, —
SIR ANDREW. So could I too.

图 11（见 82 页）

—OLIVIA'S *garden*.

Enter VIOLA, *and* Clown *with a tabor*.

VIOLA. Save thee, friend, and thy music: dost thou live by thy tabor?

CLOWN. No, sir, I live by the church.

图 12（见 106 页）

Re-enter MARIA, *with* SIR TOBY *and* FABIAN.

SIR TOBY. Which way is he, in the name of sanctity? If all the devils of hell be drawn in little, and Legion himself possessed him, yet I'll speak to him.

图 13（见 108 页）

MARIA. Get him to say his prayers, good Sir Toby, get him to pray.

MALVOLIO. My prayers, minx!

图 14（见 120—122 页）

ANTONIO.I must entreat of you some of that money.

VIOLA.What money, sir?

For the fair kindness you have show'd me here, And, part, being prompted by your present trouble,
Out of my lean and low ability
I'll lend you something: my having is not much;
I'll make division of my present with you:
Hold, there's half my coffer.

图 15（见 124 页）

FABIAN. Come, let's see the event.

SIR TOBY. I dare lay any money 'twill be nothing yet.

图 **16**（见 126 页）

— *Before* OLIVIA'S *house*.

Enter SEBASTIAN *and* CLOWN.

CLOWN. Will you make me believe that I am not sent for you?

SEBASTIAN. Go to, go to, thou art a foolish fellow: Let me be clear of thee.

图 17（见 136 页）

MALVOLIO. Believe me, I am not; I tell thee true.

CLOWN. Nay, I'll ne'er believe a madman till see his brains.

图 18（见 140 页）

OLIVIA. Then lead the way, good father;
and heavens so shine,
That they may fairly note this act of mine!

图 19（见 142 页）

Enter DUKE, VIOLA, CURIO *and* LORDS.

DUKE. Belong you to the Lady Olivia, friends?

CLOWN. Aye, sir; we are some of her trappings.

图 20（见 154 页）

CLOWN. O, he's drunk, Sir Toby, an hour agone; his eyes were set at eight i' the morning.

“莎翁戏剧经典”丛书总序

莎士比亚(William Shakespeare, 1564—1616)是英国16世纪文艺复兴时期的伟大剧作家和诗人,也是世界文坛上的巨擘。他一生创作了38部戏剧作品(一说37部),诗作包括两部长篇叙事诗、一部十四行诗集以及其他一些短篇诗作。四百多年来这些作品被翻译成多种文字,在世界各地广泛传播。正如他同时代的批评家和剧作家本·琼生所说,他是“时代的灵魂”,“不属一个时代,而属于所有的时代!”莎士比亚在世期间,他的戏剧作品曾吸引了大量观众,包括宫廷王室成员和普通百姓,产生了巨大影响。18世纪以来,这些作品始终活跃在舞台上,20世纪随着电影业的发展,它们又被搬上银幕。几百年来,无论是体现莎士比亚原作的表演还是经过不断改编的作品,莎剧都拥有众多的观者,散发出不灭的艺术光辉;另一方面,自1623年莎士比亚全集第一对开本问世,莎士比亚的戏剧也成为学者和广大普通读者阅读、学习、研究的对象,在历代读者的阅读和研究中,这些作品不断得到新阐释和挖掘。莎士比亚的作品焕发着永久不衰的生命活力。

1564年4月,莎士比亚出生于英格兰中部的埃文河畔的斯特拉福镇。家境殷实,父亲曾经营手套和羊毛,并做过小镇的镇长。莎士比亚小时曾在镇上的文法学校读书,受到过较为正规的拉丁文和古典文学的教育。不久,家道中落,陷入经济困境,这可能成为莎士比亚后来未能进入大学读书的原因。1582年,莎士比亚十八岁时与邻村一位大他八岁的女子安·哈撒韦成婚,六个月后,大女儿苏珊娜降生,此后他们又有了一对孪生子女,不幸的是,儿子哈姆内特早夭。16世纪90年代左右,莎士比亚来到伦敦,发展他的戏剧事业。他曾是剧团的演员、编剧和股东。90年代初期,莎士比亚即开始戏剧创作。1592年,莎士比亚已在同行中崭露头角，被当时的“大学才子”剧作家格林所嫉妒，他把莎士比亚称作“那只新抖起来的乌鸦”，“借我们的羽毛来打扮自己……狂妄地幻想着能独自震撼(Shake-scene)这个国家的舞台”。1592—1594年间，伦敦因流行瘟疫，大部分剧院关闭，在此期间莎士比亚完成了两部著名的长篇叙事诗《维纳斯与阿多尼斯》与《鲁克丽丝受辱记》。1594年剧院恢复营业之后，莎士比亚加入宫廷大臣剧团，并终生服务于该剧团，直到1613年离开伦敦返回家乡。90年代中期，他进入了戏剧创作的巅峰时期。在1590年至1613年的二十多年之间，莎士比亚共创作了历史剧、悲剧、喜剧、传奇剧等38部。90年代中后期，他的创作以喜剧和历史剧为主，包括喜剧《仲夏夜之梦》(1595)、《威尼斯商人》(1596)、《无事生非》(1598—1599)、《皆大欢喜》(1599—1600)等和大部分历史剧，如《理查三世》(1592—1593)、《亨利四世》(上、下)(1596—1598)、《亨利五世》(1598—1599)等。这一时期，他的创作风格较为明快，充满积极向上的格调，即便剧中有悲剧的成分，整个作品也透露出对生活的肯定，对理想的向往，如《罗密欧与朱丽叶》(1595)。进入17世纪后，莎士比亚的戏剧更多地转向对人生重大问题的思考，探索解决人生之困顿的途径，诸如权力、欲望、嫉妒、暴政等等。四大悲剧《哈姆莱特》(1600—1601)、《奥瑟罗》(1603—1604)、《李尔王》(1605—1606)、《麦克白》(1606)均完成于这一时期。此外，几部重要的罗马题材剧也在90年代末和新世纪的最初几年完成，如《裘力·凯撒》(1599)、《安东尼与克里奥佩特拉》(1606)、《科里奥兰纳斯》(1608)等。莎士比亚这一时期也创作了几部喜剧，但风格较前一时期更多悲情色彩，更为沉重而引人深思。1609年，莎士比亚《十四行诗集》出版。晚期的莎士比亚剧作风格有一定变化，最有影响的是传奇剧，如《暴风雨》，通过想象的世界与现实世界的对照来探讨人生问题。

莎士比亚的名字开始传入中国是在19世纪中上叶，他的戏剧被翻译成汉语而为国人所知则是在20世纪初期。当时，他剧作的内容通过英国19世纪兰姆姐弟《莎士比亚戏剧故事集》的汉译被介绍到中国来，即无译者署名的《澥外奇谭》(1903)和林纾、魏易翻译的《吟边燕语》(1904)。20世纪20年代，莎剧汉译事业的开拓者田汉翻译了《哈孟雷特》(1921)和《罗密欧与朱丽叶》(1924)。此后，朱生豪、梁实秋、孙大雨、曹禺、曹未风、虞尔昌等译家都翻译过莎士比亚的剧作。朱生豪先生在经历日本侵略的苦难、贫穷和疾病折磨的极其艰苦的环境下，以惊人的毅力和顽强的意志，克服种种艰难险阻，穷毕生之精力完成了31部半莎剧的翻译，成为播撒莎士比亚文明之火的普罗米修斯，译莎事业的英雄和圣徒。他的莎剧译文优美畅达，人物性格鲜明，成为广大读者所珍爱的艺术瑰宝。梁实秋是中国迄今为止唯一一位个人独立完成莎剧和莎诗汉译工程的翻译家。梁译有详尽的注释和说明，学术含量较高。1956年，卞之琳翻译的《哈姆雷特》出版，他完善了孙大雨提出的翻译原则，提出"以顿代步、韵式依原诗、等行翻译"的翻译方法，可谓开一代诗体译法之风，他的译本至今都被视作该剧最优秀的译本。方平是另一位重要的成绩卓著的莎剧翻译家。2000年由他主编主译的《新莎士比亚全集》出版，其中25部莎剧由方平翻译，其他作品由阮坤、吴兴华、汪义群、覃学岚、屠岸、张冲等译出，为国内目前首部全部由分行诗体翻译的莎剧莎诗全集。

时至今日，莎士比亚的戏剧作品仍不断有新的译本出版，对广大读者而言，阅读汉译的莎剧已经是一件十分方便的事情，而这些汉译莎剧作品中不乏优秀的译本。然而，尽管莎剧的汉译丰富多彩，莎剧的改编层出不穷，要想真正了解莎剧的本来面目，我们还须要回到莎剧原文本身。其中的原因有三：一、每一种语言都是丰富的，其表达的意义可能是多元多面的，但由于译出语和译入语两种语言之间的差异，再好的翻译也只能尽可能地贴近原文而不可能百分之百地再现原文的魅力，因此，阅读再好的译本也无法取代或等同于阅读原作；二、莎士比亚生活的时代距今已经有约400年，他所使用的英语与今天人们所熟悉的英语已有较大差异，当时的人们所熟悉的文化和历史事件也是我们今天并不熟知的，因此，要真正领悟他的作品，还须回到他那时的语言和文化中去；三、莎剧经过约400年的变迁，在改编中不断变换，有些已经走出了莎士比亚时代的莎剧，因而，想要认识和了解莎剧，最佳的办法还是回到莎剧的原文本中去。

莎士比亚生活和创作的时期在16世纪末17世纪初。英语在当时已经得到极大的发展，十分活跃而成熟，尤其莎士比亚戏剧中所运用的英语，文辞丰富、结构灵活、表达力很强。但随着时代的发展，其中的一些用词、用语以及语义等都发生了变化，与我们今天的英语存在一定距离，理解起来也就会有一定困难。莎剧在绝大多数情况下采用的是诗体写作，即人物的语言是分行的，每行十个音节，轻重音节相间，一轻一重的每两个音节构成一个音步，不押韵，因此，他的剧作均为抑扬格五音步的素体诗。这样的诗体形式突显出莎剧语言的艺术魅力，音韵优美、铿锵，节奏感强，表达生动有力。然而，正因为这是诗体写作，在语法上就可能出现诗语言特有的结构，比如倒装句或词序颠倒的现象等。莎剧的语言丰富多彩，不同人物的话语呈现出多种特色，时而体现出古典拉丁语的文风，时而出现双关语、俚语、隐喻等修辞手法。典故、历史事件、政治元素、宗教、生活习俗等等都可能成为今天的读者理解莎剧原文本的障碍。因而，借助良好的注释来理解莎剧的原作就成为我们了解和认识莎剧原貌的必要手段。这次由商务印书馆隆重推出的“莎翁戏剧经典”丛书，重点选出莎士比亚的12部经典剧作，在裘克安先生主编的“莎士比亚注释”丛书的基础上进行了改编修订，并加入了精美的插图。裘先生主编的“莎士比亚注释”丛书对莎剧原文做了多方面的详尽注释，对理解原文起到有效作用，在读者中有较广泛的影响。相信这套“莎翁戏剧经典”的出版会进一步推动莎剧在广大读者中的影响力，提高人们对阅读莎剧以及经典文学作品原文的兴趣和能力，产生积极的和广泛的影响。

屠岸 章燕

2013年10月4日

“莎士比亚注释”丛书总序

莎士比亚研究在新中国有过不平坦的道路和坎坷的命运。解放后不久，大家纷纷学俄语，学英语的人数骤减。研究英国文学，要看苏联人怎么说。“文革”十年，莎士比亚同其他西方“资产阶级”作家一样被打入冷宫。改革开放以后，1978 年人民文学出版社出版了在朱生豪译文基础上修订补足的《莎士比亚全集》。随之又出版了一些个别剧的不同译本，如方平译的《莎士比亚喜剧五种》(1979 年)和卞之琳译的《莎士比亚悲剧四种》(1988 年)。梁实秋的译本，现在大陆上也可以读到了。评介和研究莎士比亚的文章，从“文革”结束后才逐渐多起来。

但是，目前多数人学习、欣赏和研究莎士比亚，是通过中译文来进行的。精通英语而研究莎士比亚的学者不是没有，然而他们人数不多，年纪却老迈了。最近若干年，才有一些年轻人到英国或美国去学习和研究莎士比亚。

1981 年我就想到有必要在中国出版我们自己注释的莎士比亚著作。谈起来，许多朋友都赞成。1984 年中国莎士比亚研究会筹备和成立时，我自告奋勇，联系了一些志同道合的学者，共同开始编写莎士比亚注释本。商务印书馆大力支持出版这套丛书。到 2002 年底已出书 26 种，而且第一次印刷版已全部售完。这证明这套丛书是很受欢迎的。

要知道，莎士比亚是英语文学中最优秀的代表人物，他又是英语语言大师，学习、欣赏和研究他的原著，是译文无法替代的。商务印书馆以其远见卓识，早在 1910 年和 1921—1935 年间，就出版过几种莎士比亚剧本的注释本，以满足这方面的需求。那时的教会学校学生英文水平高，能读莎著；不但大学生能读，连有些中学生都能读。可从那时以后，整整 50 年中国就没印过原文的莎士比亚著作。

世界各国，莎著的注释本多得不计其数。如果唯独中国没有，实在说不过去。如果没有，对于中国知识分子欣赏和研究莎士比亚十分不利。近年来，中国人学英语的越来越多了，他们的英文水平也逐渐提高了。因此，也存在着一定的读者市场。

有了注释本，可以为明天的莎士比亚研究提供一个可靠的群众基础。而译本显然不能提供可靠的基础。

莎士比亚是16、17世纪之交的作者，他写的又是诗剧。对于现代的读者，他的英语呈现着不少的困难。不要说掌握了现代英语的中国读者，就是受过一般教育的英美人士，在初读莎士比亚原著时也面临许多障碍，需要注释的帮助。

莎士比亚的时代，英语正从受屈折变化拘束的中世纪英语，向灵活而丰富的现代英语转变。拉丁语和法语当时对英语影响很大。而莎士比亚对英语的运用又有许多革新和创造。主要的困难可以归纳为以下几个方面，也就是注释要提供帮助的方面：

（一）词汇。许多词虽然拼法和现在一样，但具有不同的早期含义，不能望文生义。另有一些词拼法和现在不一样，而含义却相同。莎士比亚独创了一些词。他特别喜欢用双关语，在他创作的早期尤其如此。而双关语是无从翻译的。这是译本无论如何也代替不了注释本的原因之一。

让我们举《哈姆莱特》剧中男主角出场后最初讲的几句话为例：

King: But now, my cousin Hamlet, and my son —
Hamlet 〔Aside〕: A little more than kin, and less than kind!
King: How is it that the clouds still hang on you?
Hamlet: Not so, my lord. I am too much i' the sun.

• 梁实秋的译文如下：

王：现在，我的侄子哈姆雷特，也是我的儿子，——
哈［旁白］：比侄子是亲些，可是还算不得儿子。
王：怎么，你脸上还是罩着一层愁云？
哈：不是的，陛下；我受的阳光太多了。

• 卞之琳的译文如下：

王：得，哈姆雷特，我的侄子，我的儿——

哈［旁白］：亲上加亲，越亲越不相亲！

王：你怎么还是让愁云惨雾罩着你？

哈：陛下，太阳大，受不了这个热劲"儿"。

• 朱生豪的译文如下：

王：可是来，我的侄儿哈姆莱特，我的孩子——

哈［旁白］：超乎寻常的亲族，漠不相干的路人。

王：为什么愁云依旧笼罩在你的身上？

哈：不，陛下；我已经在太阳里晒得太久了。

这里，主要困难在于莎士比亚让哈姆莱特使用了 kin 和 kind 以及 son 和 sun 两组双关语。kind 一词又有双关意义，翻译无法完全表达，只能各译一个侧面。结果，梁和卞两先生还得用注释补足其义，朱译则连注释也没有。这种地方，能读原文注释本的人才能充分领略莎氏原意。

哈姆莱特在旁白里说：比亲戚多一点——本来我是你的侄子，现在又成了你的儿子，确实不是一般的亲戚关系啊；然而却比 kind 少一点——kind 有两层意思，一是"同类相求"的亲近感，一是"与人为善"的善意感，我同你没有共同语言，我也不知道你是安的什么心。这话只能对自己说，在舞台上假定对方是听不到的。哈姆莱特的第二句话是公开的俏皮话：哪里有什么阴云呀，我在太阳里晒得不行呢。sun 是跟 clouds 相对；太阳又意味着国王的恩宠，"你对我太好了，我怎么会阴郁呢？"sun 又跟 son 谐音，"做你的儿子，我领教得够了。"原文并不是像梁实秋所说的那样晦涩难解。可是含义太复杂，有隐藏的深层感情，所以无法译得完全。

（二）语法。有些现象，按现代英语语法的标准看，似乎是错误的，但在当时并不错，是属于中世纪英语的残余因素。例如有些动词过去分词的词尾变化、代词的所有格形式、主谓语数的不一致、关系代词和介词的用法等方面，都有一些和现在不同的情况。注释里说明了，可以举一反三去理解。

（三）词序的颠倒和穿插。词尾屈折变化较多的中世纪英语本来对词序没有严格的要求。伊丽莎白时代继承了这种习惯。同时，诗的节律和押韵要求对词序作一定的灵活处理。莎士比亚的舞台语言以鲜明、有力、生动为首要考虑，有时他就把语法和句法放在从属的地位。在激动的台词中，由于思路、感情的变化，语言也常有脱出常规的变化。这些地方，有了注释的指点，理解就容易得多。

（四）典故。莎士比亚用典很多。古希腊、罗马神话，《圣经》故事，英国民间传说，历史逸事……他都随手拈来。其中有一大部分对于英美读者来说乃是常识，但中国读者就很需要注释的帮助。

（五）文化背景。注释可以提供关于基督教义、中世纪传统观点、文艺复兴时期新的主张、英国习俗等方面的知识。

除上述以外，还有莎剧中影射时事，以及版本考据诸问题，在注释本中可以详细论述，也可以简单提及。

世界文豪莫不是语言大师，而要真正理解和欣赏一位大师的文笔，当然非读他的原著不成。出版莎士比亚注释本，首先是为了让中国读者便于买到和读到他的原著。不过我们自知现出的几十种在版本、注释和其他方面还存在不足之处，希望读者多提意见，以便今后不断改进。

裘克安

前　　言

《第十二夜》（或《各遂所愿》）是一出五幕十八场的喜剧，约作于1601年，也就是莎士比亚以写历史剧和喜剧为主的第一创作阶段的末年。剧情曲折，而不离奇。出场人物不多，但结构紧密，全剧几无一处松弛。主题说的是伊利里亚公爵奥西诺向奥丽维娅小姐求爱，屡遭拒绝。这时有一对孪生兄妹航海到伊利里亚，在附近海上遇海难失散。妹妹薇奥拉改扮男装，投身在奥西诺公爵家中为侍童，深得奥西诺公爵的宠信，并充当代他向奥丽维娅小姐求爱的使者。奥丽维娅无意于公爵，但对女扮男装的薇奥拉却一见钟情。于是出现了三角循环的恋爱关系：奥西诺爱奥丽维娅，奥丽维娅爱薇奥拉，而薇奥拉却偷偷地爱上了奥西诺。这个循环的恋爱关系直到后来奥丽维娅碰巧遇上薇奥拉的孪生兄长西巴斯辛，两人以误就误地结成夫妇才告结束。但除了这个主题还有两个副题。一个是奥丽维娅的叔父托比爵士的朋友安德鲁爵士，由于倾心奥丽维娅，妒忌薇奥拉而引起的争风吃醋的闹剧；另一个是奥丽维娅的管家马伏里奥由于痴心梦想得到女主人的俯爱而被人愚弄的插曲。这一个主题和两个副题就像三根线，被有机地搓合在一起，拧成一股绳，做到泾渭难分，最后又同时结束。在这一点上或者可以说，莎士比亚的喜剧创作技巧在这时已达到了成熟的程度。莎士比亚对欧洲古典主义戏剧创作原则“三一律”（情节、时间、地点上的一致）一贯忽视，但在这个剧中除了时间上已超过了规定的一昼夜以外，其他两点上却达到了一致。

莎士比亚生长在英国封建制度日趋没落，资本主义制度逐渐成长，两种不同的社会制度互争消长、激烈斗争的时期。这种斗争在他的剧本中经常反映出来。在《第十二夜》中，马伏里奥的社会地位虽然只是个管家，但却象征着新兴的资产阶级。他野心勃勃，自命不凡，平时装出一副正人君子的模样，经常训人。他厌恶小丑费斯特的滑稽打趣，称他为“没有头脑的混账东西”。他看不惯托比爵士等人的腐朽生活，也听不懂他们的歌唱，称之为“直着喉咙，唱那鞋匠的歌儿”。他恃上压下，作威作福。玛丽娅把他叫作“清教徒”，并不是由于他在宗教信仰上显得比别人更虔诚，而是由于他的所作所为与当时新兴资产阶级的主要代表清教徒有些类似。托比等人之所以恨他并居心整他，一方面固然由于他对他们横加干涉，惹怒了他们，但更重要的是因为托比和安德鲁是没落封建阶级的典型代表，他们过着寄生虫般的生活，饱食终日，无所用心，除了酗酒，就是惹是生非。他们一方面留恋着这种腐朽生活，另一方面也预感到这种日子已长不了，而直接威胁着他们生存的就是马伏里奥所象征的新兴资产阶级。其实马伏里奥的妄想得到女主人的青睐，不但被剧中其他人视为“僭越”行为，对封建阶级上层人物来说更是不可思议的。奥丽维娅在垂青薇奥拉时，首先考虑到的就是家世问题。她自言自语地这样说：“你的家世怎样？……越过于我目前的境遇，但我是个有身份的人。”在奥丽维娅和西巴斯辛已经结婚的消息揭露后，公爵脱口而出的也是：“不要惊骇；他的血统也很高贵。”足见他们把维护本阶级利益时刻放在心上，而门第就是主要手段。

有人说，《第十二夜》和《威尼斯商人》有相似之处，这话也不无道理。奥西诺的自怨自艾和安东尼奥的悲观厌世有些近似，马伏里奥的老谋深算不亚于夏洛克，薇奥拉和鲍西娅都女扮男装，玛丽娅的聪明伶俐可与娜丽莎比美。看来天才如莎士比亚，在创新过程中有时也不能完全摆脱旧模子的影响。但两者比较起来，《第十二夜》读起来似乎比《威尼斯商人》使人更有轻松之感。首先，马伏里奥的最后结局不像夏洛克那样凄凉。其次，《威尼斯商人》的可笑之处主要在于夏洛克作茧自缚，害人反害己。因此在庭审一场之后就感到平淡无奇了，而《第十二夜》中的喜剧因素比较多，始终妙趣横生。奥丽维娅向薇奥拉求爱时，薇奥拉的闪烁其词已经耐人寻味，玛丽娅的巧设妙计，马伏里奥的装腔作势，狐假虎威，更使人忍俊不禁。除此以外，剧中还有几个小丑式的人物，增添了不少风趣。费斯特的插科打诨既能引人发笑，更能发人深思。托比爵士是福斯泰夫式人物，自己已经穷得寄人篱下，还不断地说大话，吹牛皮；而最可笑的是安德鲁爵士，明明胆小如鼠，却要装得气壮如牛，真叫人气不动、笑不动。全剧以兄妹团聚，情人结合告终，结束得干净利落，更增加了戏剧性。

本剧的次要角色安东尼奥船长对西巴斯辛的友情很真挚，后来错误地认为朋友辜负了他的信托，感到伤心愤懑。有论者认为这是莎士比亚自己的心声，他在十四行诗中也有同样的抱怨。这点聊供参考。

《第十二夜》以节日的笑料为主，衬以忧郁的感情，并从头至尾用音乐和歌唱来增加兴趣和气氛。编者收录了几首当时的曲谱，以供伴读或演出之用。

《第十二夜》的最早版本就是1623年收入第一对开本的本子，因此极少歧文。

从语言上讲，《第十二夜》中双关语很多，不少已在注释中注明。韵律方面，除歌曲外，以素体韵文为主，即五个抑扬格音步（十个音节）的诗行，如：

If mú|sic bé|the foód|of lóve|play ón|,

Give mé|excéss|of ít,|that súr|fei tíng|,

有时也有用双行脚韵的，特别在过场处常用。本剧中散文（对白和书信）颇多，占全剧行数一半以上。

《第十二夜》是莎士比亚著名喜剧之一，有的评论家甚至认为是他最佳的喜剧。我国北京的剧坛上曾一再上演过这个戏。戏中有许多双关语和其他文字游戏，翻译时难以译出，非读原文不识其中妙处。这个注释本作了详尽的解释，有助于读者的理解和欣赏。

在注释过程中，承老同学裘克安提供了一些资料和建议，在此表示感谢。

支荩忠

1983年9月于扬州师院

TWELFTH NIGHT

DRAMATIS PERSONAE

Orsino, Duke of Illyria
Sebastian, brother to Viola
Antonio, a sea captain, friend to Sebastian
A Sea Captain, friend to Viola
Valentine, } gentlemen attending on the Duke
Curio, } gentlemen attending on the Duke
Sir Toby Belch, uncle to Olivia
Sir Andrew Aguecheek
Malvolio, steward to Olivia
Fabian, } servants to Olivia
Clown, } servants to Olivia
Olivia
Viola, sister to Sebastian
Maria, Olivia's woman

Lords, Priests, Sailors,
Officers, Musicians,
and
other Attendants

注　　释

＊ 第十二夜，指圣诞节后的第十二夜，即 1 月 6 日夜，又称 Feast of the Epiphany 耶稣对三博士显圣宴，它既是基督教圣诞节假日的最后一天，又和古罗马 Saturnalia 农神节的传统有关。但这剧不一定是为 1 月 6 日夜演出用。莎士比亚时代，“第十二”译作 twelfe，这就是本剧剧名在最早的第一对开本(1623)中的译法。

List of Characters：

＊ **Orsino** [ɔːˈsiːnəu]：1601 年 1 月 6 日(第十二夜)伊丽莎白女王曾接待意大利佛罗伦萨的布拉契阿诺大公奥西诺，此名可能莎士比亚从他借来。

＊ **Illyria** [iˈliriə]：伊利里亚，欧洲古地名，位于巴尔干半岛亚得里亚海边，在今阿尔巴尼亚。**Duke of Illyria**：伊利里亚大公。

＊ **Valentine** [ˈvæləntəin] .

＊ **Curio** [ˈkjuəriəu] .

＊ **Viola** [ˈvaiələ] .

＊ **Cesario** [siːˈzɑːriəu] .

＊ **Sebastian** [siˈbæstjən] .

＊ **Antonio** [ænˈtəuniəu] .

＊ **Olivia** [əˈliviə]：countess，女伯爵。

＊ **Maria** [məˈraiə] .

＊ **Aguecheek** [ˈeigjuːtʃiːk]：意为寒颤病的面颊。**protégé** [ˈprəuteʒei]：〈法语〉被保护人。

＊ **Malvolio** [mælˈvəuljəu]：一说意大利语中 Mal volio 意为 I want Mall. 据考证，Mall 指伊丽莎白宫廷女侍从 Mary Fitton，其保护人 Sir William Knollys 对她迷恋和垂涎。Malvolio 即影射 Knollys.

＊ **Fabian** [ˈfeibjən] .

＊ **Feste** [ˈfest] .

ACT I

SCENE I

—An apartment in the DUKE'S *palace.*

Enter DUKE, CURIO, *and other* LORDS; MUSICIANS *attending.*]

DUKE. If music be the food of love, play on;
Give me excess of it, that, surfeiting,
The appetite may sicken, and so die.
That strain again! it had a dying fall:
O, It came o'er my ear like the sweet sound,
That breathes upon a bank of violets,
Stealing and giving odor! Enough; no more:
'Tis not so sweet now as it was before.
O spirit of love, how quick and fresh art thou!
That, notwithstanding thy capacity
Receiveth as the sea, nought enters there,
Of what validity and pitch soe'er,
But falls into abatement and low price,
Even in a minute! so full of shapes is fancy,
That it alone is high fantastical.

CURIO. Will you go hunt, my lord?

DUKE. What, Curio?

CURIO. The hart.

DUKE. Why, so I do, the noblest that I have:
O, when mine eyes did see Olivia first,
Methought she purged the air of pestilence!
That instant was I turn'd into a hart;
And my desires, like fell and cruel hounds,
E'er since pursue me.

I. i （第一幕第一场，后类推）（以下黑体数字为行码）

2 **that**：so that. **surfeiting**：being overfed.

3 **appetite**：longing (for music).

4 **strain**：tune. **fall**：cadence，收束音。

5 **o'er**：over.

7 **odor**：sweet smell.

9 **quick and fresh**：keen and eager (to devour). **art thou**：you are. thou 旧时和诗体中第二人称单数代词，art 是 be 的第二人称单数现在时形式。

10 **That**：in that. **notwithstanding**：although. **thy**：your 第二人称单数代词所有格。

11 **Receiveth**：receives 旧时英国北部动词第三人称单数现在时的结尾用 -th 的形式，在莎剧中 -s 和 -th 的形式混用。

11—13 **nought enters... But falls**：nothing enters... that does not fall. **But**：that not. **there**：into your capacity (into the sea).

12 **what... soe'er**：whatsoever. **validity**：value. **pitch**：excellence.

13 **abatement**：depreciation，贬值。

14 **fancy**：love.

15 **alone**：all-one，above all things，exceeding all other passions. **high fantastical**：highly imaginative.

16 **hunt**：不定式省略 to，现在习惯说 go hunting.

18 **hart**：鹿和 heart 同音，双关。

19 **so I do**：I do want to go hunt the hart. **the noblest that I have**：the hart (heart) I have in mind is the noblest，指 Olivia 的心。

20 **mine**：my. 诗中 my 在元音前时常换用 mine，因其易读。

21 伊丽莎白时代常发生鼠疫，当时不知病源，以为有一种瘟疫的空气，室内用香草的烟熏过，即可净化空气。

23—24 参考奥维德《变形记》中述希腊神话，猎人 Actaeon 无意见到月神黛安娜裸体出浴，被罚化为鹿，并为他自己的猎狗群撕咬致死。**fell**：fierce. **pursue**：has pursued and is pursuing.

Enter VALENTINE.]

How now! what news from her?

VALENTINE. So please my lord, I might not be admitted;
But from her handmaid do return this answer:
The element itself, till seven years' heat,
Shall not behold her face at ample view;
But, like a cloistress, she will veilèd walk
And water once a day her chamber round
With eye-offending brine: all this to season
A brother's dead love, which she would keep fresh
And lasting in her sad remembrance.

DUKE. O, she that hath a heart of that fine frame
To pay this debt of love but to a brother,
How will she love, when the rich golden shaft
Hath kill'd the flock of all affections else
That live in her; when liver, brain and heart,
These sovereign thrones, are all supplied, and fill'd
Her sweet perfections with one self king!
Away before me to sweet beds of flowers:
Love-thoughts lie rich when canopied with bowers.

[*Exeunt*.

SCENE II

—The sea-coast.

Enter VIOLA, a CAPTAIN, *and* SAILORS.]

VIOLA. What country, friends, is this?

CAPTAIN. This is Illyria, lady.

VIOLA. And what should I do in Illyria?
My brother he is in Elysium.
Perchance he is not drown'd: what think you, sailors?

CAPTAIN. It is perchance that you yourself were saved.

VIOLA. O my poor brother! and so perchance may he be.

CAPTAIN. True, madam: and, to comfort you with chance,

26 **So please**:if it please ... so. **might not be**:could not be,was not permitted to be.

27 **return**:bring back.

28 **The element**:the sky. **till seven years' heat**:until seven summers have passed.

29 **at ample view**:in full view.

30 **veilèd**:è 上加撇,表明这个 è 要读音。

31 **round** (prep.):all over (her chamber).

32 **eye-offending brine**:stinging tears. **season** (v. t.):用盐腌,使之不腐。

35 **that fine frame**:such a fine nature.

36 **To**:as to. **but**:only,merely.

37 **shaft**:(小爱神丘比特的)arrow.

38 **all affections else**:all the other emotions.

39 **liver,brain and heart**:seats (thrones) of passion,judgement and sentiments.

41 **self**:same. 这里 king 指 Orsino 自己。当时流行的观念认为,男子占据妇女的心(all supplied and filled with one king),妇女才能达到完美的境地(perfections).

42 **Away before me**:lead the way.

42—43 这两行行尾押韵。在一场和一幕之末常常如此,以示小结。

Exeunt. [拉丁语,'eksiʌnt]:下场(第三人称复数现在时)。

I. ii

4 **Elysium**:(希腊神话中的)乐土,天堂。

5 **Perchance**:perhaps 在下行中则解 by chance,by luck.

8 **chance**:possibility of good (or bad) fortune.

Assure yourself, after our ship did split,
When you and those poor number saved with you
Hung on our driving boat, I saw your brother,
Most provident in peril, bind himself,
Courage and hope both teaching him the practice,
To a strong mast that lived upon the sea;
Where, like Arion on the dolphin's back,
I saw him hold acquaintance with the waves
So long as I could see.

VIOLA. For saying so, there's gold:
Mine own escape unfoldeth to my hope,
Whereto thy speech serves for authority,
The like of him. Know'st thou this country?

CAPTAIN. Aye, madam, well; for I was bred and born
Not three hours' travel from this very place.

VIOLA. Who governs here?

CAPTAIN. A noble Duke, in nature as in name.

VIOLA. What is his name?

CAPTAIN. Orsino.

VIOLA. Orsino! I have heard my father name him:
He was a bachelor then.

CAPTAIN. And so is now, or was so very late;
For but a month ago I went from hence,
And then 'twas fresh in murmur, — as, you know,
What great ones do the less will prattle of, —
That he did seek the love of fair Olivia.

VIOLA. What's she?

CAPTAIN. A virtuous maid, the daughter of a count
That died some twelvemonth since; then leaving her
In the protection of his son, her brother,
Who shortly also died: for whose dear love,
They say, she hath abjured the company
And sight of men.

VIOLA. O that I served that lady,

10 **poor number**: few.

11 **Hung**: hang. **driving**: being forced along.

12 **provident**: prudent.

14 **lived**: kept afloat (水手用语)。

15 **Arion** [ə'raiən]:公元前七世纪希腊音乐家,传说在他竞赛后携奖品返程时,贪财的船员将他掷入海中,后为海豚所救。

16 **hold acquaintance with**: bob up and down with.

18 **there's gold**: Viola 说此句时给船长金币,作为酬谢。

19—21 **unfoldeth to my hope, . . . The like of him**: encourages me in my hope that the same should happen to him. 这里 of = as regards.

20 **Whereto**: to which (my hope). **authority**: grounds,根据。

30 **late**: recent.

31 **but**: only.

32 **murmur**: rumour.

33 **great ones**: great men. **the less**: those of lower rank.

37 **since**: ago.

39 **for**: in memory of.

40 **abjured**: vowed to shun.

42 **that I served that lady**: served 是假定式,表示愿望。that I might serve that lady 或 how happy I would be if I could serve that lady.

And might not be delivered to the world,
Till I had made mine own occasion mellow,
What my estate is!

CAPTAIN. That were hard to compass;
Because she will admit no kind of suit,
No, not the Duke's.

VIOLA. There is a fair behavior in thee, captain;
And though that nature with a beauteous wall
Doth oft close in pollution, yet of thee
I will believe thou hast a mind that suits
With this thy fair and outward character.
I prithee, and I'll pay thee bounteously,
Conceal me what I am, and be my aid
For such disguise as haply shall become
The form of my intent. I'll serve this Duke:
Thou shalt present me as an eunuch to him:
It may be worth thy pains; for I can sing,
And speak to him in many sorts of music,
That will allow me very worth his service.
What else may hap to time I will commit;
Only shape thou thy silence to my wit.

CAPTAIN. Be you his eunuch, and your mute I'll be:
When my tongue blabs, then let mine eyes not see.

VIOLA. I thank thee: lead me on.

[*Exeunt*.

SCENE III

—OLIVIA'S *house*.

Enter SIR TOBY BELCH *and* MARIA.]

SIR TOBY. What a plague means my niece, to take the death of her brother thus? I am sure care's an enemy to life.

MARIA. By my troth, Sir Toby, you must come in earlier

43 **delivered**: revealed.

44 **had made**（假定式）**mine own occasion mellow**: have decided that the time is ripe.

45 **estate**: status.

46 **were**: would be. **compass**: bring about.

47 **admit ... suit**: accept petition.

49 **thee**: thou 的受格。

50—51 **though** 从句: though nature often encloses pollution (evil thinking) with a beauteous wall (pretty personal appearance). **though that**: though. **of thee**: about you.

53 **outward character**: face or features.

54 **prithee**: pray you.

55 **Conceal me what I am**: conceal my identity. 这里 me 是重复的宾语。

56 **haply**: perhaps. **become**: suit.

57 **The form of my intent**: the purpose which I have shaped.

59 **pains**: trouble, effort.

61 **allow me**: approve me as being. **worth**: valuable to.

62 **hap**: happen. **to time I will commit**: I will entrust to time.

63 **shape**: adjust. **wit**: design.

64 **mute**: dumb attendant. 当时东方和意大利贵族,确有用阉人和哑巴做侍者的。

I. iii

1 **What a plague**: 一种咒骂语,类似"他妈的"。

2 **care**: sorrow.

4 **troth**: truth, faith. **By my troth**: on my word (一种咒骂语)。

o'nights: your cousin, my lady, takes great exceptions to your ill hours.

SIR TOBY. Why, let her except, before excepted.

MARLA. Aye, but you must confine yourself within the modest limits of order.

SIR TOBY. Confine! I'll confine myself no finer than I am: these clothes are good enough to drink in; and so be these boots too: an they be not, let them hang themselves in their own straps.

MARIA. That quaffing and drinking will undo you: I heard my lady talk of it yesterday; and of a foolish knight that you brought in one night here to be her wooer.

SIR TOBY. Who, Sir Andrew Aguecheek?

MARIA. Aye, he.

SIR TOBY. He's as tall a man as any's in Illyria.

MARIA. What's that to the purpose?

SIR TOBY. Why, he has three thousand ducats a year.

MARIA. Aye, but he'll have but a year in all these ducats; he's a very fool and a prodigal.

SIR TOBY. Fie, that you'll say so! he plays o'the viol-de-gamboys, and speaks three or four languages word for word without book, and hath all the good gifts of nature.

MARIA. He hath indeed, almost natural: for besides that he's a fool, he's a great quarreler: and but that he hath the gift of a coward to allay the gust he hath in quarreling, 'tis thought among the prudent he would quickly have the gift of a grave.

SIR TOBY. By this hand, they are scoundrels and subtractors that say so of him. Who are they?

MARIA. They that add, moreover, he's drunk nightly in your company.

SIR TOBY. With drinking healths to my niece: I'll drink to her as long as there is a passage in my throat and drink

5—6 o'nights:on nights,晚上常常。 **cousin**:伊丽莎白时代泛指亲戚。按上文说,Olivia 是他的 niece. **takes great exceptions to**:objects very much to.

6 ill hours:late hours.

7 except, before excepted(法律用语):exceptis excipiendis 的变形,意为 object to what she objected to before. 推论的意思是"她过去没反对,现在为什么要反对?"

8 confine:keep.

12 an:if.

14 undo:ruin.

19 tall:英勇。下行 Maria 则理解为一般的"身材高大"。**any's**:any who is.

21 ducats [ˈdʌkəts]:欧洲旧时一种金币,约合三分之一英镑。

22 but:only. 这句意思,他所有的钱,一年之内都会花光的。

23 very:complete.

24—25 Fie:呸。**viol-de-gamboys**:base-viol,低音小提琴。

28 natural:half-witted.

29 but that:if ... not. 这里 gift 是"天赋",下面的 gift 是"白得的礼物"。

30 gust:taste, relish,嗜好。

33—34 By this hand:凭我的手起誓。**subtractors**:是 detractors(诋毁者)的误用形式,表示 Sir Toby 爱用大词,而学问不足。

35 nightly:every night.

in Illyria: he's a coward and a coystrill that will not drink to my niece till his brains turn o' the toe like a parish-top. What, wench! Castiliano vulgo; for here comes Sir Andrew Agueface.

Enter SIR ANDREW AGUECHEEK.]

SIR ANDREW. Sir Toby Belch! how now, Sir Toby Belch!

SIR TOBY. Sweet Sir Andrew!

SIR ANDREW. Bless you, fair shrew.

MARIA. And you too, sir.

SIR TOBY. Accost, Sir Andrew, accost.

SIR ANDREW. What's that?

SIR TOBY. My niece's chambermaid.

SIR ANDREW. Good Mistress Accost, I desire better acquaintance.

MARIA. My name is Mary, sir.

SIR ANDREW. Good Mistress Mary Accost,—

SIR TOBY. You mistake, knight: 'accost' is front her, board her, woo her, assail her.

SIR ANDREW. By my troth, I would not undertake her in this company. Is that the meaning of 'accost'?

MARIA. Fare you well, gentlemen.

SIR TOBY. An thou let part so, Sir Andrew, would thou mightst never draw sword again.

SIR ANDREW. An you part so, mistress, I would I might never draw sword again. Fair lady, do you think you have fools in hand?

MARIA. Sir, I have not you by the hand.

SIR ANDREW. Marry, but you shall have; and here's my hand.

MARIA. Now, sir, 'thought is free': I pray you, bring your hand to the buttery-bar and let it drink.

SIR ANDREW. Wherefore, sweetheart? what's your metaphor?

MARIA. It's dry, sir.

39 **coystrill** (coistrel):mean fellow.

40 **turn**:spin. **o' the**:on the.

41 **parish-top**:whipping-top kept for the exercise of parishioners. **Castiliano vulgo**:Castiliano 是 1600 年一个剧本里一个魔鬼的名字,vulgo 意为“俗话说”。这句话类似“说到曹操,曹操就到”。

47 **Accost**:原意是船和船“靠拢”,转义“搭话”。Sir Andrew 不懂这字,以为是 Maria 的名字。

54—55 **'accost' is front her, / board her, ...**:To accost her is to front her,board her.... **front**:迎面驶去。 **board**:登船。这两个动词和 assail (进攻)都是船员用语,但 board her 和 assail her 又有对女子强行非礼之义,故 Sir Andrew 有下面这句话。

56—57 **undertake**:engage with. **in this company**:when there are people about.

59 **An thou let part so**:if you let her go away like this (part=depart). **would**:I would,I wish.

60 **draw sword**:act like a man.

63 **in hand**:to deal with.

64 **by the hand**:拉住手。这里用 hand 做文字游戏。

65 **Marry** (interj.):by Mary (一种轻微的赌咒语)。

67 **'thought is free'**:every one has a right to his opinion. 这是俗话,暗指“你是傻瓜”。

68 **buttery-bar**:酒店柜台。

69 **Wherefore**:to what end,for what purpose.

71 这里用 dry 做文字游戏,此字至少有下列各义:①干;②渴;③乏味;④ dry hand 还暗指阳痿。

SIR ANDREW. Why, I think so: I am not such an ass but I can keep my hand dry. But what's your jest?

MARIA. A dry jest, sir.

SIR ANDREW. Are you full of them?

MARIA. Aye, sir, I have them at my fingers' end: marry, now I let go your hand, I am barren. [*Exit*.

SIR TOBY. O knight, thou lackest a cup of canary: when did I see thee so put down?

SIR ANDREW. Never in your life, I think; unless you see canary put me down. Methinks sometimes I have no more wit than a Christian or an ordinary man has: but I am a great eater of beef and I believe that does harm to my wit.

SIR TOBY. No question.

SIR ANDREW. An I thought that, I'ld forswear it. I'll ride home to-morrow, Sir Toby.

SIR TOBY. Pourquoi, my dear knight?

SIR ANDREW. What is 'pourquoi'? do or not do? I would I had bestowed that time in the tongues that I have in fencing, dancing and bear-baiting: O, had I but followed the arts!

SIR TOBY. Then hadst thou had an excellent head of hair.

SIR ANDREW. Why, would that have mended my hair?

SIR TOBY. Past question; for thou seest it will not curl by nature.

SIR ANDREW. But it becomes me well enough, does't not?

SIR TOBY. Excellent; it hangs like flax on a distaff; and I hope to see a housewife take thee between her legs and spin it off.

SIR ANDREW. Faith, I'll home to-morrow, Sir Toby: your niece will not be seen; or if she be, it's four to one she'll none of me: the count himself here hard by woos her.

SIR TOBY. She'll none o' the count: she'll not match above her degree, neither in estate, years, nor wit; I have

72 **but**: that,(成语) Fools have wit enough to keep themselves dry.

77 **now I let go your hand, I am barren**: 指示 You are the origin of all my jests.

78 **lackest**: lack (旧时第二人称单数的谓语字尾有 -est). **canary**: 加那利 (Canary [kəˈnɛəri]) 群岛所产的葡萄酒。

79 **put down**: 这里解"斗嘴时被击败",下面解"使昏醉"。

86 **I'ld forswear it**: I would make a vow never to eat beef again.

88 **Pourquoi** 〈法语〉: why.

89 **I would**: I wish.

90 **tongues**: languages.

91 **bear-baiting**: 用狗斗熊是当时一种流行的游戏。 **followed**: engaged in the pursuit of.

93 这里玩弄同音词游戏: tongues (学语言) 和 tongs (卷发钳) 同音。**hadst thou had**: you would have had. **an excellent head of hair**: a head of excellent hair. 英语口语中现在还有这种说法,例如把 a cup of nice tea 说成 a nice cup of tea.

94 **that**: my following the arts. **mended**: improved.

95—96 **Past question**: beyond question. **by nature**: naturally.

98—100 伊丽莎白时代认为性病和纵欲能使人过早秃顶。

101 **Faith**: in faith. **I'll home**: I will go home.

102—103 **four to one**: 四比一的可能性,即可能性不小。**she'll none of me**: she will have none of me (she will not marry me).

heard her swear 't. Tut, there's life in 't, man.

SIR ANDREW. I'll stay a month longer. I am a fellow o' the strangest mind i' the world; I delight in masques and revels sometimes altogether.

SIR TOBY. Art thou good at these kickshawses, knight?

SIR ANDREW. As any man in Illyria, whatsoever he be, under the degree of my betters; and yet I will not compare with an old man.

SIR TOBY. What is thy excellence in a galliard, knight?

SIR ANDREW. Faith, I can cut a caper.

SIR TOBY. And I can cut the mutton to 't.

SIR ANDREW. And I think I have the back-trick simply as strong as any man in Illyria.

SIR TOBY. Wherefore are these things hid? wherefore have these gifts a curtain before 'em? are they like to take dust, like Mistress Mall's picture? why dost thou not go to church in a galliard and come home in a coranto? My very walk should be a jig; I would not so much as make water but in a sink-a-pace. What dost thou mean? Is it a world to hide virtues in? I did think, by the excellent constitution of thy leg, it was formed under the star of a galliard.

SIR ANDREW. Aye, 'tis strong, and it does indifferent well in a flame-colored stock. Shall we set about some revels?

SIR TOBY. What shall we do else? were we not born under Taurus?

SIR ANDREW. Taurus! That's sides and heart.

SIR TOBY. No, sir; it is legs and thighs. Let me see thee caper: ha! higher: ha, ha! excellent! [*Exeunt*.

106 Tut (interj.)：嘿。**there's life in 't**：it's not yet hopeless. **man**：fellow，chap.

108—109 masques and revels：伊丽莎白时代宫廷和贵族最喜爱的哑剧、化装舞会等娱乐方式。

110 kickshawses（从法语 quelques choses 变来）：trifles，玩意儿。

112 betters：social superiors.

113 old man：old hand.

114 galliard：16、17 世纪流行的一种活泼的五步舞，第五步要跳跃一下，即下面说的 cut a caper.

115 caper：吃羊肉时的一种调味料，因此 Sir Toby 又谈起羊肉。

116 to 't：to match it，相称。

117 back-trick：①舞蹈中后退的一跳；②腰功。

120—121 like：likely. **take dust**：gather dust，影射名誉玷污。

121 Mall：指宫廷女侍从 Mary Fitton，参见本剧首 Malvolio 注。她和 1601 年一件宫廷丑闻有关。

122 coranto：a quick dance.

123 jig：a quick，lively dance.

124 sink-a-pace（法语 cinquepas）：另一种五步舞，sink 又可作"下水道"解。

126 constitution：frame，shape.

128 indifferent：fairly，tolerably.

132 Taurus（拉丁语，意为公牛）：金牛座。欧洲古占星术中说，十二星座分管人体的部位，金牛为第二星座，主管颈部和喉咙。

133 sides and heart：腰部和心脏。

SCENE IV

—*The* DUKE'S *palace*.

Enter VALENTINE, *and* VIOLA *in man's attire*.]

VALENTINE. If the Duke continue these favors towards you, Cesario, you are like to be much advanced: he hath known you but three days, annd already you are no stranger.

VIOLA. You either fear his humor or my negligence, that you call in question the continuance of his love: is he inconstant, sir, in his favors?

VALENTINE. No, believe me.

VIOLA. I thank you. Here comes the count.

Enter DUKE, CURIO, *and* ATTENDANTS.]

DUKE. Who saw Cesario, ho?

VIOLA. On your attendance, my lord; here.

DUKE. Stand you a while aloof. Cesario,
Thou know'st no less but all; I have unclasp'd
To thee the book even of my secret soul:
Therefore, good youth, address thy gait unto her;
Be not denied access, stand at her doors,
And tell them, there thy fixed foot shall grow
Till thou have audience.

VIOLA. Sure, my noble lord,
If she be so abandon'd to her sorrow
As it is spoke, she never will admit me.

DUKE. Be clamorous and leap all civil bounds
Rather than make unprofited return.

VIOLA. Say I do speak with her, my lord, what then?

DUKE. O, then unfold the passion of my love,
Surprise her with discourse of my dear faith:
It shall become thee well to act my woes;
She will attend it better in thy youth

I. iv

2 **Cesario**: the assumed name of Viola. **advanced**: promoted.

5 **humor**: fickleness. **that**: in that.

12 **aloof**: at a distance.

13 **no less but all**: all, everything. **but**: than. **unclasp'd**: opened. 旧时手抄书有用金属钩扣合者。

15 **address thy gait unto**: direct your steps towards.

16 **denied**: refused. **access**: admittance.

17 **grow**: take root.

18 **audience**: interview.

21 **spoke**: spoken, said.

22 **leap**: overstep.

24 **Say I do speak with her**: suppose I do have the chance to speak with her. **what then**?: what am I to do then?

25 **unfold**: disclose, reveal. **passion**: fervor.

26 **discourse**: account. **dear**: heartfelt. **faith**: loyalty.

28 **attend**: attend to, heed.

Than in a nuncio's of more grave aspect.
VIOLA. I think not so, my lord.
DUKE. Dear lad, believe it;
For they shall yet belie thy happy years,
That say thou art a man; Diana's lip
Is not more smooth and rubious; thy small pipe
Is as the maiden's organ, shrill and sound;
And all is semblative a woman's part.
I know thy constellation is right apt
For this affair. Some four or five attend him;
All, if you will; for I myself am best
When least in company. Prosper well in this,
And thou shalt live as freely as thy lord,
To call his fortunes thine.
VIOLA. I'll do my best
To woo your lady: [*Aside*] yet, a barful strife!
Whoe'er I woo, myself would be his wife. [*Exeunt*.

SCENE V

—OLIVIA'S *house*.

Enter MARIA *and* CLOWN.]

MARIA. Nay, either tell me where thou hast been, or I will not open my lips so wide as a bristle may enter in way of thy excuse: my lady will hang thee for thy absence.

CLOWN. Let her hang me: he that is well hanged in this world needs to fear no colors.

MARIA. Make that good.

CLOWN. He shall see none to fear.

MARIA. A good lenten answer: I can tell thee where that saying was born, of 'I fear no colors.'

CLOWN. Where, good Mistress Mary?

MARIA. In the wars; and that may you be bold to say in your foolery.

29 Than in a nuncio's of more grave aspect: Than in = that of; nuncio = envoy; aspect = appearance.

32—33 此句可意译如下:For those who say that you are a man will fail to give the idea of your tender youth.

34 **rubious**: ruby-colored. **pipe**: voice, vocal chord.

35 **organ**: vocal organ. **sound**: unbroken.

36 **semblative**: like, resembling.

37 **constellation**: a person's character which is determined by the star under which he was born. **right** (adv.): just, exactly. **apt**: fit, suitable.

38 **Some**: 一句系对仆从讲的。

39 **All, if you will**: You may all go with him, if you wish to.

41—42 此句 To call 短语移位,等于说 you will be as free to use my fortunes as I am. **fortunes**: a person's possessions, wealth.

44 ***Aside***: 旁白。 **a barful strife!**: a struggle waged for the purpose of hindering it from attaining success.

I. v

2—3 **in** (by) **way of thy excuse**: to make excuse for you.

5 **colors**: ①军旗(指敌人);②颈圈(和 collars 同音)。

6 **Make that good**: make yourself clear.

8 **lenten**: meager, thin, 平淡无味的。

11—12 **and that may you be bold to say in your foolery**: and now that you know where that saying was born, you may boldly say it in your foolery.

CLOWN. Well, God give them wisdom that have it; and those that are fools, let them use their talents.

MARIA. Yet you will be hanged for being so long absent; or, to be turned away, is not that as good as a hanging to you?

CLOWN. Many a good hanging prevents a bad marriage; and, for turning away, let summer bear it out.

MARIA. You are resolute, then?

CLOWN. Not so, neither; but I am resolved on two points.

MARIA. That if one break, the other will hold; or, if both break, your gaskins fall.

CLOWN. Apt, in good faith; very apt. Well, go thy way; if Sir Toby would leave drinking, thou wert as witty a piece of Eve's flesh as any in Illyria.

MARIA. Peace, you rogue, no more o' that. Here comes my lady: make your excuse wisely, you were best.

[*Exit*.

CLOWN. Wit, an 't be thy will, put me into good fooling! Those wits, that think they have thee, do very oft prove fools; and I, that am sure I lack thee, may pass for a wise man: for what says Quinapalus? 'Better a witty fool than a foolish wit.'

Enter LADY OLIVIA *with* MALVOLIO.]

God bless thee, lady.

OLIVIA. Take the fool away.

CLOWN. Do you not hear, fellows? Take away the lady.

OLIVIA. Go to, you're a dry fool; I'll no more of you: besides, you grow dishonest.

CLOWN. Two faults, madonna, that drink and good counsel will amend: for give the dry fool drink, then is the fool not dry: bid the dishonest man mend himself; if he mend, he is no longer dishonest; if he cannot, let the botcher mend him. Any thing that's mended is but patched: virtue that transgresses is but patched with

19 **let summer bear it out**:may the fine weather hold.

21 **resolved**:firm. **points**:①点;②一种把裤子连接于上衣的襻带。

23 **gaskins**:breeches.

25 **leave drinking**:戒酒。**thou wert**:you should be.

26 **a piece of Eve's flesh**:a girl. 暗示 Maria 和 Sir Toby 可以配对。

28 **you were best**:it would be best for you(were 是假定式)。

29 **an 't be thy will**:if it be your will.

30 **wits**:smart fellows.

32 **Quinapalus**:the name of a nonexistent man,杜撰的人名。

37 **Go to**:去你的吧(表示不赞成,不耐烦)。 **dry**:stupid,dull. **I'll no more of you**:I'll have no more to do with you.

39 **Two faults**:i. e.,being a dry fool and being dishonest. **madonna**〈意大利语〉:my lady,madam.

40 **amend**:cure,improve.

41 **mend**:①reform;②repair.

43 **botcher**:tailor who does repairs.

44 **transgresses**:sins,errs.

sin; and sin that amends is but patched with virtue. If that this simple syllogism will serve, so; if it will not, what remedy? As there is no true cuckold but calamity, so beauty's a flower. The lady bade take away the fool; therefore I say again, take her away.

OLIVIA. Sir, I bade them take away you.

CLOWN. Misprision in the highest degree! Lady, cucullus non facit monachum; that's as much to say as I wear not motley in my brain, Good madonna, give me leave to prove you a fool.

OLIVIA. Can you do it?

CLOWN. Dexteriously, good madonna.

OLIVIA. Make your proof.

CLOWN. I must catechize you for it, madonna: good my mouse of virtue, answer me.

OLIVIA. Well, sir, for want of other idleness, I'll bide your proof.

CLOWN. Good madonna, why mournest thou?

OLIVIA. Good fool, for my brother's death.

CLOWN. I think his soul is in hell, madonna.

OLIVIA. I know his soul is in heaven, fool.

CLOWN. The more fool, madonna, to mourn for your brother's soul being in heaven. Take away the fool, gentlemen.

OLIVIA. What think you of this fool, Malvolio? doth he not mend?

MALVOLIO. Yes, and shall do till the pangs of death shake him; infirmity, that decays the wise, doth ever make the better fool.

CLOWN. God send you, sir, a speedy infirmity, for the better increasing your folly! Sir Toby will be sworn that I am no fox; but he will not pass his word for two pence that you are no fool.

OLIVIA. How say you to that, Malvolio?

45—46 **If that**:if. **syllogism**:逻辑学中的三段论法。 **so**:good, very well.

47—48 **what remedy?**:what is there to be done? **calamity**:misfortune.

51—52 **Misprision**:①wrongful arrest;②misunderstanding. **cucullus non facit monachum**(拉丁成语):戴上僧帽并不就成为僧侣。

52—53 **I wear not motley in my brain**:Wearing a fool's clothes doesn't make me a fool. **motley**:parti-colored dress of a professional fool,职业小丑穿的彩衣。 **leave**:permission.

56 **Dexteriously**:dexterously.

58 **good my**:my good.

59 **mouse**:playful term of endearment for a little girl.

60 **want**:lack. **idleness**:amusement. **bide**:abide,wait for.

61 **proof**:test.

66 **The more fool**:you are a fool all the more.

72 **decays**(v. t.):harms,damages.

74—75 **for the better increasing**:in order the better to increase.

76—77 **fox**:a crafty person. **pass**:pledge. **for two pence**:用两便士作赌注。

MALVOLIO. I marvel your ladyship takes delight in such a barren rascal: I saw him put down the other day with an ordinary fool that has no more brain than a stone. Look you now, he's out of his guard already; unless you laugh and minister occasion to him, he is gagged. I protest , I take these wise men , that crow so at these set kind of fools, no better than the fools' zanies.

OLIVIA. O, you are sick of self-love, Malvolio, and taste with a distempered appetite. To be generous, guiltless and of free disposition, is to take those things for bird-bolts that you deem cannon-bullets: there is no slander in an allowed fool, though he do nothing but rail; nor no railing in a known discreet man, though he do nothing but reprove.

CLOWN. Now Mercury endue thee with leasing, for thou speakest well of fools!

Re-enter MARIA.]

MARIA. Madam, there is at the gate a young gentleman much desires to speak with you.

OLIVIA. From the Count Orsino, is it?

MARIA. I know not, madam: 'tis a fair young man, and well-attended.

OLIVIA. Who of my people hold him in delay?

MARIA. Sir Toby, madam, your kinsman.

OLIVIA. Fetch him off, I pray you; he speaks nothing but madman: fie on him! [*Exit* MARIA. Go you, Malvolio: if it be a suit from the count, I am sick, or not at home; what you will, to dismiss it. [*Exit* MALVOLIO. Now you see, sir, how your fooling grows old, and people dislike it.

CLOWN. Thou hast spoke for us, madonna, as if thy eldest son should be a fool; whose skull Jove cram with brains! for,— here he comes,— one of thy kin has a most weak pia mater.

79 **I marvel**: I am surprised that.

80 **barren**: dull, unresponsive. **rascal**: fellow（贬义不如现在重）。 **put** (p. p.) **down ... with**: snubbed by, defeated in repartee by.

81 **stone**: ①石头;②当时确有一丑角名 Stone.

82 **out of his guard**: defenceless.（击剑用语）

83 **minister**: give. **occasion**: opportunity for attacking. **gagged**: silenced.

84 **protest**: declare. **take**: regard, consider. **crow**: laugh gleefully.

85 **set**: stereotyped, not spontaneous. **zanies**: stooges, 类似捧哏。

86 **you are sick of self-love**: you have the fault of being too conceited.

87 **distempered**: diseased, ailing. **guiltless**: guileless, 坦率的。

88—89 **free**: magnanimous. **bird-bolts**: blunt-headed arrows for shooting birds. **cannon-bullets**: cannon-balls.

90—91 **allowed**: approved, licensed, professional. **nor no railing**: 这种双重否定词的用法,在当时常见。

93 **Mercury**: 古罗马神话中骗子和窃贼之神。 **endue**: endow. **leasing**: lying.

95 **gentleman**: 之后省略 who.

99 **well-attended**: with several attendants.

100 **hold him in delay**: are detaining him.

102 **but**: except like a.

104 **suit**: plea for love. **I**: 前省略 say.

108 **spoke**: spoken.

109 **Jove**: 罗马神话中的天神 Jupiter. 这类用 Jove 的地方,莎士比亚原来写的都可能是 God,由于 1606 年 5 月 27 日颁布舞台上禁用渎神语言的法律而后改的。 **Jove cram**: may Jove cram.

111 **pia mater**〈拉丁语〉: brain.

Enter SIR TOBY.]

OLIVIA. By mine honor, half drunk. What is he at the gate, cousin?

SIR TOBY. A gentleman.

OLIVIA. A gentleman! what gentleman?

SIR TOBY. 'Tis a gentleman here—a plague o' these pickle-herring! How now, sot!

CLOWN. Good Sir Toby!

OLIVIA. Cousin, cousin, how have you come so early by this lethargy?

SIR TOBY. Lechery! I defy lechery. There's one at the gate.

OLIVIA. Aye, marry, what is he?

SIR TOBY. Let him be the devil, an he will, I care not: give me faith, say I. Well, it's all one. [*Exit*.

OLIVIA. What's a drunken man like, fool?

CLOWN. Like a drowned man, a fool and a mad man: one draught above heat makes him a fool; the second mads him; and a third drowns him.

OLIVIA. Go thou and seek the crowner, and let him sit o' my coz; for he's in the third degree of drink, he's drowned: go look after him.

CLOWN. He is but mad yet, madonna; annd the fool shall look to the madman. [*Exit*.

Re-enter MALVOLIO.]

MALVOLIO. Madam, yond young fellow swears he will speak with you. I told him you were sick; he takes on him to understand so much, and therefore comes to speak with you. I told him you were asleep; he seems to have a foreknowledge of that too, and therefore comes to speak with you. What is to be said to him, lady? he's fortified against any denial.

OLIVIA. Tell him he shall not speak with me.

MALVOLIO. Has been told so; and he says, he'll stand at your door like a sheriff's post, and be the supporter to

112 he: the man.

116 a plague o': a plague on 一种诅咒语，相当于"该死"。酒醉的 Sir Toby 此时反胃打嗝，故咒骂他吃过的腌鱼。

117 sot: fool.

119 come . . . by: get.

120 lethargy: torpor，昏沉状态。

121 Lechery!: lust!（他把 lethargy 错听成 lechery）

123—124 an: if. **give me faith**: believe me.

127 heat: normal temperature.

129—130 crowner: coroner，验尸官。**sit o'**: sit on，hold an inquest of.

130 coz: cousin 在这里也是通指亲戚。

133 look to: look after.

135—136 he takes on him: he professes. **therefore**: for that reason.

140 he's fortified against: he is impervious to.

142 Has: he has.

143 sheriff's post: 地方行政长官门前立有一柱，作为权力的象征。

a bench, but he'll speak with you.

OLIVIA. What kind o' man is he?

MALVOLIO. Why, of mankind.

OLIVIA. What manner of man?

MALVOLIO. Of very ill manner: he'll speak with you, will you or no.

OLIVIA. Of what personage and years is he?

MALVOLIO. Not yet old enough for a man, nor young enough for a boy; as a squash is before 'tis a peascod, or a codling when 'tis almost an apple: 'tis with him in standing water, between boy and man. He is very well-favored and he speaks very shrewishly; one would think his mother's milk were scarce out of him.

OLIVIA. Let him approach: call in my gentlewoman.

MALVOLIO. Gentlewoman, my lady calls. [*Exit*.

Re-enter MARIA.]

OLIVIA. Give me my veil: come, throw it o'er my face.
We'll once more hear Orsino's embassy.

Enter VIOLA, *and* ATTENDANTS.]

VIOLA. The honorable lady of the house, which is she?

OLIVIA. Speak to me; I shall answer for her. Your will?

VIOLA. Most radiant, exquisite and unmatchable beauty, —I pray you, tell me if this be the lady of the house, for I never saw her: I would be loath to cast away my speech, for besides that it is excellently well penned, I have taken great pains to con it. Good beauties, let me sustain no scorn; I am very comptible, even to the least sinister usage.

OLIVIA. Whence came you, sir?

VIOLA. I can say little more than I have studied, and that question's out of my part. Good gentle one, give me modest assurance if you be the lady of the house, that I may proceed in my speech.

OLIVIA. Are you a comedian?

147 **manner**: kind, sort.

148 **manner**: manners, bearing, deportment.

149 **no**: not.

150 **personage**: personal appearance.

152 **squash**: unripe pea-pod,嫩豆荚。 **peascod**:熟豆荚。

153 **codling**:生苹果。

154 **standing water**:既未涨潮也未落潮时的一般水位。

155 **well-favored**: good-looking.

160 **embassy**: message.

162 **Your will**?: What is your pleasure?

166 **penned**: written.

167 **con**: learn by heart.

168—169 **comptible**: susceptible, sensitive. **sinister usage**: unfair treatment, slight.

172 **out of my part**: not included in my prepared speech.

VIOLA. No, my profound heart: and yet, by the very fangs of malice I swear, I am not that I play. Are you the lady of the house?

OLIVIA. If I do not usurp myself, I am.

VIOLA. Most certain, if you are she, you do usurp yourself; for what is yours to bestow is not yours to reserve. But this is from my commission: I will on with my speech in your praise, and then show you the heart of my message.

OLIVIA. Come to what is important in 't: I forgive you the praise.

VIOLA. Alas, I took great pains to study it, and 'tis poetical.

OLIVIA. It is the more like to be feigned. I pray you, keep it in. I heard you were saucy at my gates, and allowed your approach rather to wonder at you than to hear you. If you be not mad, be gone; if you have reason, be brief; 'tis not that time of moon with me to make one in so skipping a dialogue.

MARIA. Will you hoist sail, sir? here lies your way.

VIOLA. No, good swabber; I am to hull here a little longer. Some mollification for your giant, sweet lady. Tell me your mind: I am a messenger.

OLIVIA. Sure, you have some hideous matter to deliver, when the courtesy of it is so fearful. Speak your office.

VIOLA. It alone concerns your ear. I bring no overture of war, no taxation of homage: I hold the olive in my hand; my words are as full of peace as matter.

OLIVIA. Yet you began rudely. What are you? what would you?

VIOLA. The rudeness that hath appeared in me have I learned from my entertainment. What I am, and what I would, are as secret as maiden-head; to your ears, divinity, to any other's, profanation.

176 — 177 profound: difficult to fathom. **fangs**: canine teeth (here used in a figurative sense). **by the very fangs of malice I swear**: let me be bitten to death if I don't tell the truth.

177 I am not that I play:I am not what I appear to be.

179 usurp: counterfeit. 下行 Viola 取其另一义 exercise a power which is not yours by right.

181 what is yours to bestow is not yours to reserve: You have no right to reserve what is in your power to give.

182 from:away from,departing from. **on with**:go on with.

183 heart:essence.

185 forgive:excuse (from delivering).

189 like:likely.

191 wonder at:have a look at.

193—194 'tis not that time of moon with me:I am not sufficiently lunatic. 古罗马人认为月亮影响神志,满月能使一些人疯狂;lunatic 即从拉丁文 luna (月亮)变来。 **make one in**: take part in. **skipping**: flighty,thoughtless.

195 hoist sail:depart,扬帆。Maria 借用航海术语,下一行 Viola 也照办。

196 swabber:(船上负责打扫、擦洗的)水手。 **hull**: drift with sails furled,逗留。

197 Some mollification for:pray, pacify. **your giant**:称 Maria 巨人是反话,她身材矮小。这句话是转向 Olivia 说的。

200 courtesy:greetings,introduction. **fearful**:alarming(指 Viola 曾在门口吵嚷)。 **office**:mission.

201 It alone concerns your ear:It is for you alone to hear. **overture**:proposal.

202 taxation:demand. **olive**:橄榄枝(和平的象征)。

203 matter:sense,substance.

207 my entertainment:the way in which I have been received. 这里 entertainment 是被动式动名词。

OLIVIA. Give us the place alone: we will hear this divinity. [*Exeunt* MARIA *and* ATTENDANTS.] Now, sir, what is your text?

VIOLA. Most sweet lady,—

OLIVIA. A comfortable doctrine, and much may be said of it. Where lies your text?

VIOLA. In Orsino's bosom.

OLIVIA. In his bosom! In what chapter of his bosom?

VIOLA. To answer by the method, in the first of his heart.

OLIVIA. O, I have read it: it is heresy. Have you no more to say?

VIOLA. Good madam, let me see your face.

OLIVIA. Have you any commission from your lord to negotiate with my face? You are now out of your text: but we will draw the curtain and show you the picture. Look you, sir, such a one I was this present: is 't not well done?

[*Unveiling*.

VIOLA. Excellently done, if God did all.

OLIVIA. 'Tis in grain, sir; 'twill endure wind and weather.

VIOLA. 'Tis beauty truly blent, whose red and white
Nature's own sweet and cunning hand laid on:
Lady, you are the cruel'st she alive,
If you will lead these graces to the grave
And leave the world no copy.

OLIVIA. O, sir, I will not be so hard-hearted; I will give out divers schedules of my beauty: it shall be inventoried, and every particle and utensil labeled to my will: as, item, two lips, indifferent red; item, two gray eyes, with lids to them; item, one neck, one chin, and so forth. Were you sent hither to praise me?

VIOLA. I see you what you are, you are too proud;
But, if you were the devil, you are fair.

212 **text**:牧师讲道时一般先引用的一段《圣经》上的经文。

214 **comfortable**:comforting. **doctrine**:topic of a sermon(这里指 Most sweet lady).

218 **by the method**:in the same style. **the first**:the first chapter.

225 **this present**:just now. 此处 Olivia 揭开自己的面纱。

227 **if God did all**:if it is natural.

228 **in grain**:ingrained.

229 **truly**:properly, masterfully. **blent**:blended.

230 **cunning**:clever, skilful.

231 **she**:woman.

233 **leave the world no copy**:leave no offspring.

235—236 **schedules**:lists of the details. **inventoried**:catalogued, 列出盘货单。**particle**:item. **labeled** (v. t.):attached as a 'label' or codicil(遗嘱的附录)。

237 **as**:namely. **indifferent** (adv.):tolerably, fairly.

239 **praise**:appraise, estimate.

240 **I see you what you are**:第一个 you 为重复的补语。

My lord and master loves you: O, such love
Could be but recompensed, though you were crown'd
The nonpareil of beauty!
OLIVIA. How does he love me?
VIOLA. With adorations, fertile tears,
With groans that thunder love, with sighs of fire.
OLIVIA. Your lord does know my mind; I cannot love him:
Yet I suppose him virtuous, know him noble,
Of great estate, of fresh and stainless youth;
In voices well divulged, free, learn'd and valiant;
And in dimension and the shape of nature
A gracious person: but yet I cannot love him;
He might have took his answer long ago.
VIOLA. If I did love you in my master's flame,
With such a suffering, such a deadly life,
In your denial I would find no sense;
I would not understand it.
OLIVIA. Why, what would you?
VIOLA. Make me a willow cabin at your gate,
And call upon my soul within the house;
Write loyal cantons of contemned love
And sing them loud even in the dead of night;
Halloo your name to the reverberate hills,
And make the babbling gossip of the air
Cry out 'Olivia!' O, you should not rest
Between the elements of air and earth,
But you should pity me!
OLIVIA. You might do much.
What is your parentage?
VIOLA. Above my fortunes, yet my state is well:
I am a gentleman.
OLIVIA. Get you to your lord;
I cannot love him: let him send no more;
Unless, perchance, you come to me again,

244 **nonpareil**：unmatched one.

246 **fertile**：abundant.

247 **thunder** (v. t.)：loudly declare.

252 **In voices well divulged**：well spoken of. **free**：of noble character.

253 **in dimension and the shape of nature**：in stature and personal appearance.

254 **gracious**：attractive.

255 **He might have took his answer long ago**：He might have taken my refusal as the final answer long ago.

256 **flame**：fervor.

257 **deadly**：death-like.

258 **In your denial I would find no sense**：I would find your denial unreasonable.

260 **what would you**?：what would you do?

261 **Make me**：(I will) make for myself. **willow**：杨柳(象征被拒绝的爱情)。

262 **my soul**：指 Olivia.

263 **cantons**：cantos，songs.

265 **Halloo**：shout. **reverberate**：echoing，reverberating.

266 **babbling gossip**：echo (拟人化，gossip 意为饶舌者)。

269—270 **But**：unless. **do**：achieve.

272 **state**：social standing.

To tell me how he takes it. Fare you well:
I thank you for your pains: spend this for me.

VIOLA. I am no fee'd post, lady; keep your purse:
My master, not myself, lacks recompense.
Love make his heart of flint that you shall love;
And let your fervor, like my master's, be
Placed in contempt! Farewell, fair cruelty. [*Exit*.

OLIVIA. 'What is your parentage?'
'Above my fortunes, yet my state is well:
I am a gentleman.' I'll be sworn thou art;
Thy tongue, thy face, thy limbs, actions, and spirit,
Do give thee five-fold blazon: not too fast: soft, soft!
Unless the master were the man. How now!
Even so quickly may one catch the plague?
Methinks I feel this youth's perfections
With an invisible and subtle stealth
To creep in at mine eyes. Well, let it be.
What ho, Malvolio!

Re-enter MALVOLIO.]

MALVOLIO. Here, madam, at your service.

OLIVIA. Run after that same peevish messenger,
The county's man: he left this ring behind him,
Would I or not: tell him I'll none of it.
Desire him not to flatter with his lord,
Nor hold him up with hopes; I am not for him:
If that the youth will come this way to-morrow,
I'll give him reasons for 't; hie thee, Malvolio.

MALVOLIO. Madam, I will. [*Exit*.

OLIVIA. I do I know not what, and fear to find
Mine eye too great a flatterer for my mind.
Fate, show thy force: ourselves we do not owe;
What is decreed must be, and be this so. [*Exit*.

278 **spend this for me**:此处 Olivia 要给 Viola 一些赏钱。

279 **fee'd post**:messenger to be tipped.

281 May the God of Love make the heart of the man whom you will love hard as flint.

287—288 Your tongue, face, limbs, actions and spirit (altogether five features) all testify to your being of high birth. **blazon**:贵族的纹章。**soft** (adv.):stay, stop. Olivia 告诫自己不要太快地爱上 Viola.

289 **man**:servant.

290 **the plague**:传染病,喻爱情。

297 **county**:count,伯爵。

298 **Would I or not**:whether I would take it or not. **I'll none of it**:I'll have none of it.

299 **flatter with**:deal flatteringly with, encourage.

301 **If that**:if.

302 **hie thee**:make haste.

305 **eye too great a flatterer for my mind**:眼睛对我的理智来说是太大的谄媚者;意思是我把 Viola 的外表看得太好了,超越了理智。

306 **owe**:own, control.

ACT II

SCENE I

— The sea-coast.

Enter ANTONIO *and* SEBASTIAN.]

ANTONIO. Will you stay no longer? nor will you not that I go with you?

SEBASTIAN. By your patience, no. My stars shine darkly over me: the malignancy of my fate might perhaps distemper yours; therefore I shall crave of you your leave that I may bear my evils alone: it were a bad recompense for your love, to lay any of them on you.

ANTONIO. Let me yet know of you whither you are bound.

SEBASTIAN. No, sooth, sir: my determinate voyage is mere extravagancy. But I perceive in you so excellent a touch of modesty, that you will not extort from me what I am willing to keep in; therefore it charges me in manners the rather to express myself. You must know of me then, Antonio , my name is Sebastian, which I called Roderigo. My father was that Sebastian of Messaline, whom I know you have heard of. He left behind him myself and a sister, both born in an hour: if the heavens had been pleased, would we had so ended! but you, sir, altered that; for some hour before you took me from the breach of the sea was my sister drowned.

ANTONIO. Alas the day.

SEBASTIAN. A lady, sir, though it was said she much resembled me, was yet of many accounted beautiful: but, though I could not with such estimable wonder overfar

II. i

1—2 nor will you not that I go: or do you not want me to go.

3—4 patience: leave, permission. **My stars shine darkly over me**: I am down on my luck; I am out of luck.

4 malignancy: evil influence (an astrological term).

5 distemper (v.): disturb. **crave**: beg.

6 leave: permission. **evils**: misfortune. **it were** (假定式): it would be.

7 them: evils (misfortune). **lay . . . on**: impose on.

8 yet: nevertheless. **of you**: from you.

9 sooth: indeed. **determinate**: intended.

10—11 But I can see that you are so modest that you would not force me to tell you what I want to keep secret. **extravagancy**: wandering about.

12 charges me: calls on me. **in manners**: becomely, decently.

13 the rather: the more readily. **express**: reveal.

18 so: in the same manner (i. e., in an hour, 同时)。

20 breach: breakers. **was my sister**: my sister was, 倒装。

22 Alas the day: alas.

24 of many: by many people.

25 could not: should not. **estimable wonder**: admiring judgement.

believe that, yet thus far I will boldly publish her; she bore a mind that envy could not but call fair. She is drowned already, sir, with salt water, though I seem to drown her remembrance again with more.

ANTONIO. Pardon me, sir, your bad entertainment.

SEBASTIAN. O good Antonio, forgive me your trouble.

ANTONIO. If you will not murder me for my love, let me be your servant.

SEBASTIAN. If you will not undo what you have done, that is, kill him whom you have recovered, desire it not. Fare ye well at once: my bosom is full of kindness, and I am yet so near the manners of my mother, that upon the least occasion more mine eyes will tell tales of me. I am bound to the Count Orsino's court: farewell.

[*Exit*.

ANTONIO. The gentleness of all the gods go with thee!
I have many enemies in Orsino's court,
Else would I very shortly see thee there.
But, come what may, I do adore thee so,
That danger shall seem sport, and I will go. [*Exit*.

SCENE II

—*A street*.

Enter VIOLA, MALVOLIO *following*.]

MALVOLIO. Were not you even now with the Countess Olivia?

VIOLA. Even now, sir; on a moderate pace I have since arrived but hither.

MALVOLIO. She returns this ring to you, sir: you might have saved me my pains, to have taken it away yourself. She adds, moreover, that you should put your lord into a desperate assurance she will none of him: and one thing more, that you be never so hardy to come again

25—26 overfar / believe that: have too much belief in that. **boldly**: with confidence. **publish her**: say of her.

29 her remembrance: her memory，对她的怀念。 **with more**: with tears.

30 your bad entertainment: the fact that you have not been entertained well by me. 注意：此处 entertainment 取其被动意义。

31 your trouble: the trouble I have caused you.

32 murder me for my love: cause me to die of grief at leaving you.

35 kill him whom you have recovered: kill me whom you have rescued. **desire**: request. **it**: to be my servant. 此句等于说，I would rather die than letting you demean yourself by waiting on me.

37—38 so near the manners of my mother: so like my mother. **upon the least occasion**: for the slightest reason. **tell tales of me**: betray my feelings (by shedding tears).

39 bound to: bound for，going to.

40 gentleness: blessing.

42 Else: otherwise.

43 so: 和下行的 That 呼应。

44 will: am determined.

II. ii

1 even now: just now.

3—4 on a moderate pace: as I walk rather slowly. **since**: since I left her. **arrived but hither**: come only this far.

6—7 pains: trouble (of coming after you). **to have taken it away yourself**: 此句为简略了的条件从句，相当于 if you had taken it away yourself.

8 desperate assurance: certainty beyond hope. **will none of him**: will have nothing to do with him.

9 hardy: obdurate，执拗。

in his affairs, unless it be to report your lord's taking of this. Receive it so.

VIOLA. She took the ring of me: I'll none of it.

MALVOLIO. Come, sir, you peevishly threw it to her; and her will is, it should be so returned: if it be worth stooping for, there it lies in your eye; if not, be it his that finds it. [*Exit*.

VIOLA. I left no ring with her: what means this lady?
Fortune forbid my outside have not charm'd her!
She made good view of me: indeed, so much,
That methought her eyes had lost her tongue,
For she did speak in starts distractedly.
She loves me, sure; the cunning of her passion
Invites me in this churlish messenger.
None of my lord's ring! why, he sent her none.
I am the man: if it be so, as 'tis,
Poor lady, she were better love a dream.
Disguise, I see, thou art a wickedness,
Wherein the pregnant enemy does much.
How easy is it for the proper-false
In women's waxen hearts to set their forms!
Alas, our frailty is the cause, not we!
For such as we are made of, such we be.
How will this fadge? my master loves her dearly;
And I, poor monster, fond as much on him;
And she, mistaken, seems to dote on me.
What will become of this? As I am man,
My state is desperate for my master's love;
As I am woman,—now alas the day! —
What thriftless sighs shall poor Olivia breathe!
O time! thou must untangle this, not I;
It is too hard a knot for me to untie! [*Exit*.

10—11 **in his affairs**: on his errand. **taking of this**: reaction to this message.

12 **of**: from.

13 **Come**: relent, be reasonable. **peevishly**: obstinately.

14 **so**: in the same manner. 接着他就把戒指掷在地上。

15 **eye**: view, sight.

18 **Fortune forbid**: let fortune forbid. **outside**: appearance.

19 **made good view of me**: eyed me closely.

20 **methought**: it seemed to me. **lost**: made her lose.

21 **in starts**: by fits and starts, 不连贯地。

22 **cunning of her passion**: craftiness inspired by her love.

23 **Invites me in this churlish messenger**: makes her to extend an invitation to me through this churlish messenger.

25 **I am the man**: I am the man she is in love with.

26 **she were better**: it would be better for her to.

28 **pregnant**: resourceful. **enemy**: devil.

29 **proper-false**: handsome deceiver.

30 **waxen**: easily impressed. **set their forms**: make their impressions.

31 **we**: women in general.

32 Since women are made of wax, they are impressionable.

33 **fadge**: turn out.

34 **fond** (v.): dote.

37 **My state is desperate for my master's love**: There is no hope for me to have my master's love.

39 **thriftless**: useless.

40 **untangle this**: unravel this knot.

SCENE III

—OLIVIA'S *house*.

Enter SIR TOBY *and* SIR ANDREW.]

SIR TOBY. Approach, Sir Andrew: not to be abed after midnight is to be up betimes; and 'diluculo surgere,' thou know'st,—

SIR ANDREW. Nay, by my troth, I know not: but I know, to be up late is to be up late.

SIR TOBY. A false conclusion: I hate it as an unfilled can. To be up after midnight and to go to bed then, is early: so that to go to bed after midnight is to go to bed betimes. Does not our life consist of the four elements?

SIR ANDREW. Faith, so they say; but I think it rather consists of eating and drinking.

SIR TOBY. Thou 'rt a scholar; let us therefore eat and drink. Marian, I say! a stoup of wine!

Enter CLOWN.]

SIR ANDREW. Here comes the fool, i' faith.

CLOWN. How now, my hearts! did you never see the picture of 'we three'?

SIR TOBY. Welcome, ass. Now let's have a catch.

SIR ANDREW. By my troth, the fool has an excellent breast. I had rather than forty shillings I had such a leg, and so sweet a breath to sing, as the fool has. In sooth, thou wast in very gracious fooling last night, when thou spokest of Pigrogromitus, of the Vapians passing the equinoctial of Queubus: 'twas very good, i' faith. I sent thee sixpence for thy leman: hadst it?

CLOWN. I did impeticos thy gratillity; for Malvolio's nose is no whipstock: my lady has a white hand, and the Myrmidons are no bottle-ale houses.

II. iii

2 **betimes**: early. **diluculo surgere**〈拉丁语〉:全文为 Diluculo surgere saluberrimum est,意为“早起对身体有益”。

4 **troth**: truth, faith. **by my troth**:起誓词。

9 **four elements**: earth, water, air and fire (中世纪哲学认为一切物体都由这四种元素构成)。

13 **stoup**: measure for liquor (= 2 quarts).

16 **'we three'**:当时流行的幻觉画。一人从一头看去是个小丑,第二人从另一头看去是另一个小丑,第三人走来问“我在哪里?”他从侧面看去画上是头驴。

17 **catch**:轮唱曲,小曲。

18 **breast**: pair of lungs, voice.

19 **I had rather than forty shillings I had such a leg, ...**: I would rather have such a leg ... than forty shillings. leg 指类似演员谢幕时弯腿鞠躬的姿势。

21 **gracious**: elegant, lovely.

22—23 这里是小丑随口编的假天文学名词。

24 **leman**: sweetheart.

25 **impeticos**:丑角说的滑稽话,可能是“inpocket(放进口袋)”一字说走了样。 **gratillity**: gratuity, tip.

26 **whipstock**:鞭柄。这句话可能说马伏里奥的鼻子是弯的,嗅觉灵敏,善于闻出哪里有钱。 **my lady**:即上文的 thy leman (情妇)。**white hand**:可能指滥花钱。

27 **Myrmidons**:可能是 Mermaidens 的谐音,酒店名。这句可能说这酒店善骗钱。以上四句话的意思没有确切的连贯解释,可能都是说他为什么把赏钱藏了起来。

SIR ANDREW. Excellent! why, this is the best fooling, when all is done. Now, a song.

SIR TOBY. Come on; there is sixpence for you: let's have a song.

SIR ANDREW. There's a testril of me, too: if one knight give a —

CLOWN. Would you have a love-song, or a song of good life?

SIR TOBY. A love-song, a love-song.

SIR ANDREW. Aye, aye: I care not for good life.

CLOWN. [*Sings*]

O mistress mine, where are you roaming?
O, stay and hear; your true love's coming,
That can sing both high and low:
Trip no further, pretty sweeting;
Journeys end in lovers meeting,
Every wise man's son doth know.

SIR ANDREW. Excellent good, i' faith.

SIR TOBY. Good, good.

CLOWN. [*Sings*]

What is love? 'tis not hereafter;
Present mirth hath present laughter;
What's to come is still unsure:
In delay there lies no plenty;
Then come kiss me, sweet and twenty,
Youth's a stuff will not endure.

SIR ANDREW. A mellifluous voice, as I am true knight.

SIR TOBY. A contagious breath.

SIR ANDREW. Very sweet and contagious, i' faith.

SIR TOBY. To hear by the nose, it is dulcet in contagion. But shall we make the welkin dance indeed? shall we rouse the night-owl in a catch that will draw three souls out of one weaver? shall we do that?

SIR ANDREW. An you love me, let's do't. I am dog at a

32 **testril**:tester 或 teston(面值为一先令的古钱币,在莎士比亚时只值六便士)。 **of me**:from me.

34—35 **song of good life**:drinking song. 但 37 行的 good life 指善行。

38 歌一,见 170 页。

40 **love**:paramour,情郎。

42 **Trip**:make a journey. **sweeting**:darling.

44 **wise man's son**:fool,(成语) Wise men have fools for their sons.

52 **sweet and twenty**:term of endearment (twenty times sweet).

53 **stuff**:后省略 which.

55 **contagious**:①catchy;②foul-smelling.

57 **dulcet**:sweet-sounding.

58 **welkin**:sky.

59 **in a catch**:by a song. **three souls**:motion,feeling and sense.

60 **weaver**:当时英国纺织匠多为欧洲逃亡来的加尔文派新教徒(影响了英国的清教徒),他们在听到好的赞美诗时,常现出一种狂喜出神的表情,不动不响,像丧失了三魂七魄似的。这是一处莎士比亚对清教徒进行轻微嘲笑的地方。

61 **An**:if. **dog**:铁搭钩。

catch.

CLOWN. By 'r lady, sir, and some dogs will catch well.

SIR ANDREW. Most certain. Let our catch be, 'Thou knave.'

CLOWN. 'Hold thy peace, thou knave,' knight? I shall be constrained in 't to call thee knave, knight.

SIR ANDREW. 'Tis not the first time I have constrained one to call me knave. Begin, fool: it begins 'Hold thy peace.'

CLOWN. I shall never begin if I hold my peace.

SIR ANDREW. Good, i' faith. Come, begin. [*Catch sung. Enter* MARIA.]

MARIA. What a caterwauling do you keep here! If my lady have not called up her steward Malvolio and bid him turn you out of doors, never trust me.

SIR TOBY. My lady's a Cataian, we are politicians, Malvolio 's a Peg-a-Ramsey, and 'Three merry men be we.' Am not I consanguineous? am I not of her blood? Tillyvally. Lady! [*Sings*] 'There dwelt a man in Babylon, lady, lady!'

CLOWN. Beshrew me, the knight's in admirable fooling.

SIR ANDREW. Aye, he does well enough if he be disposed, and so do I too: he does it with a better grace, but I do it more natural.

SIR TOBY. [*Sings*] 'O, the twelfth day of December,' —

MARIA. For the love o' God, peace!

Enter MALVOLIO.]

MALVOLIO. My masters, are you mad? or what are you? Have you no wit, manners, nor honesty, but to gabble like tinkers at this time of night? Do ye make an alehouse of my lady's house, that ye squeak out your coziers' catches without any mitigation or remorse of voice? Is there no respect of place, persons, nor time in you?

62 **catch**:门、窗、箱的扣锁、把手等。

63 **By 'r lady**:by our Lady,a mild oath. **catch** (v.):①扣搭;②捉拿。

66 歌二,见 171 页。

68 **constrained**:forced.

73 **caterwauling**:cat's screaming.

76 **Cataian**:从中世纪拉丁文 Cat(h)aya 变来,意为契丹人、中国人,转意为“难以猜透的人”。 **politicians**:schemers.

77—78 **Peg-a-Ramsey**:民谣中一个嫉妒和惯于偷听、偷看妻子的名字。**'Three merry men be we'**:歌三,见 172 页。 **consanguineous**:of the same blood.

79—80 **Tillyvally**:expression of impatience. **'There dwelt a man in Babylon,lady,lady!'**:歌曲名,关于《圣经铁书》中苏珊娜的故事。

81 **Beshrew**:curse.

82 **disposed**:in a merry mood.

88 **wit**:sense. **honesty**:decency.

91 **coziers**:cobblers. **mitigation**:lowering. **remorse**:intermission.

92 **respect**:consideration.

SIR TOBY. We did keep time, sir, in our catches. Sneck up!

MALVOLIO. Sir Toby, I must be round with you. My lady bade me tell you, that, though she harbors you as her kinsman, she 's nothing allied to your disorders. If you can separate yourself and your misdemeanors, you are welcome to the house; if not, an it would please you to take leave of her, she is very willing to bid you farewell.

SIR TOBY. 'Farewell, dear heart, since I must needs be gone.'

MARIA. Nay, good Sir Toby.

CLOWN. 'His eyes do show his days are almost done.'

MALVOLIO. Is 't even so?

SIR TOBY. 'But I will never die.'

CLOWN. Sir Toby, there you lie.

MALVOLIO. This is much credit to you.

SIR TOBY. 'Shall I bid him go?'

CLOWN. 'What an if you do?'

SIR TOBY. 'Shall I bid him go, and spare not?'

CLOWN. 'O no, no, no, no, you dare not.'

SIR TOBY. Out o' tune, sir: ye lie. Art any more than a steward? Dost thou think, because thou art virtuous, there shall be no more cakes and ale?

CLOWN. Yes, by Saint Anne, and ginger shall be hot i' the mouth too.

SIR TOBY. Thou 'rt i' the right. Go, sir, rub your chain with crums. A stoup of wine, Maria!

MALVOLIO. Mistress Mary, if you prized my lady's favor at any thing more than contempt, you would not give means for this uncivil rule: she shall know of it, by this hand. [*Exit*.

MARIA. Go shake your ears.

SIR ANDREW. 'Twere as good a deed as to drink when a man 's a-hungry, to challenge him the field, and then to

94 Sneck up! :go hang!

95 round:plain-spoken,blunt.

96 harbors (v.):lodges.

97 nothing allied to your disorders:in no way bound to put up with your disorderly acts.

98 separate yourself and your misdemeanors: rid yourself of your misdemeanors.

99 an:if.

102 歌四,见 173 页。

111 an if:even if.

114 Art... :art thou,are you?

116 cakes and ale:教会宴会时传统的饮食,为清教徒所反对。

117 by Saint Anne:I swear by Saint Anne,mother of the Virgin Mary. 这也是清教徒不愿意听的名字。

119—120 rub your chain with crums:用面包屑擦饰链,指马伏里奥在奥莉维娅家地位低微。

121—122 at any thing more than contempt:not as anything beneath contempt.

122—123 give means for:supply the means for,pander to. **uncivil rule**:disorderly conduct. **she**:Olivia.

123—124 by this hand:I swear by my hand,you may be sure.

125 Go shake your ears:go and make the best of things (like a dog when wet).

126 'Twere:it would be.

127 a-hungry:hungry. **challenge him the field**:challenge him to a duel.

break promise with him and make a fool of him.

SIR TOBY. Do 't, knight: I'll write thee a challenge; or I'll deliver thy indignation to him by word of mouth.

MARIA. Sweet Sir Toby, be patient for to-night: since the youth of the count's was to-day with my lady, she is much out of quiet. For Monsieur Malvolio, let me alone with him: if I do not gull him into a nayword, and make him a common recreation, do not think I have wit enough to lie straight in my bed; I know I can do it.

SIR TOBY. Possess us, possess us; tell us something of him.

MARIA. Marry, sir, sometimes he is a kind of puritan.

SIR ANDREW. O, if I thought that, I'ld beat him like a dog!

SIR TOBY. What, for being a puritan? thy exquisite reason, dear knight?

SIR ANDREW. I have no exquisite reason for 't, but I have reason good enough.

MARIA. The devil a puritan that he is, or any thing constantly, but a time-pleaser; an affectioned ass, that cons state without book and utters it by great swarths: the best persuaded of himself, so crammed, as he thinks, with excellencies, that it is his grounds of faith that all that look on him love him; and on that vice in him will my revenge find notable cause to work.

SIR TOBY. What wilt thou do?

MARIA. I will drop in his way some obscure epistles of love; wherein, by the color of his beard, the shape of his leg, the manner of his gait, the expressure of his eye, forehead, and complexion, he shall find himself most feelingly personated. I can write very like my lady your niece: on a forgotten matter we can hardly make distinction of our hands.

SIR TOBY. Excellent! I smell a device.

SIR ANDREW. I have't in my nose too.

130 deliver: report.

133 out of quiet: disquieted，心烦意乱。 **For**: as for.

134 gull: dupe, cheat. **nayword**: byword, proverb.

135 common recreation: source of amusement for everybody.

138 Possess: tell.

145 The devil a puritan that he is: how the devil can he be a puritan!

146 time-pleaser: time-server，趋权附势之徒。 **affectioned**: affected，装腔作势的。 **cons** (v.): learns.

147—148 state: high-sounding phrases to show one's grandeur. **without book**: from memory, by rote. **swarths**: heaps. **the best persuaded of himself**: the most conceited.

149 grounds: basis, foundation.

155 expressure: expression.

157 feelingly: appropriately. **personated**: represented, described.

159 of: between.

SIR TOBY. He shall think, by the letters that thou wilt drop, that they come from my niece, and that she 's in love with him.

MARIA. My purpose is, indeed, a horse of that color.

SIR ANDREW. And your horse now would make him an ass.

MARIA. Ass, I doubt not.

SIR ANDREW. O, 'twill be admirable!

MARIA. Sport royal, I warrant you: I know my physic will work with him. I will plant you two, and let the fool make a third, where he shall find the letter: observe his construction of it. For this night, to bed, and dream on the event. Farewell. [*Exit*.

SIR TOBY. Good night, Penthesilea.

SIR ANDREW. Before me, she 's a good wench.

SIR TOBY. She 's a beagle, true-bred, and one that adores me: what o' that?

SIR ANDREW. I was adored once too.

SIR TOBY. Let 's to bed, knight. Thou hadst need send for more money.

SIR ANDREW. If I cannot recover your niece, I am a foul way out.

SIR TOBY. Send for money, knight; if thou hast her not i' the end, call me cut.

SIR ANDREW. If I do not, never trust me, take it how you will.

SIR TOBY. Come, come, I'll go burn some sack; 'tis too late to go to bed now: come, knight; come, knight.

[*Exeunt*.

SCENE IV

—*The* DUKE'S *palace*.

Enter DUKE, VIOLA, CURIO, *and others*.]

DUKE. Give me some music. Now, good morrow, friends,

165 **a horse of that color**: something of that kind.

170 **Sport royal**: splendid jest. **physic**: medicine (to purge Malvolio's conceit).

171 **work with**: act upon. **plant**: to place under cover for the purpose of spying.

173 **construction**: interpretation.

175 **Penthesilea**: an Amazonian queen, a commanding woman.

176 **Before me**: upon my soul,我敢发誓说。

177 **beagle**:小猎犬。 **true-bred**: pure-bred,纯种的。

180 **Let 's to bed**: Let's go to bed.

182—183 **recover**: get hold of. **a foul way out**: bankrupt.

185 **cut**: a common working horse, applied contemptuously to a man,笨蛋。

188 **burn some sack**: warm and spice some Spanish wine.

II. iv

1 **good morrow**: good morning.

Now, good Cesario, but that piece of song,
That old and antique song we heard last night:
Methought it did relieve my passion much,
More than light airs and recollected terms
Of these most brisk and giddy-paced times:
Come, but one verse.

CURIO. He is not here, so please your lordship, that should sing it.

DUKE. Who was it?

CURIO. Feste, the jester, my lord; a fool that the lady Olivia's father took much delight in. He is about the house.

DUKE. Seek him out, and play the tune the while.

[*Exit* CURIO. *Music plays*.

Come hither, boy: if ever thou shalt love,
In the sweet pangs of it remember me;
For such as I am all true lovers are,
Unstaid and skittish in all motions else,
Save in the constant image of the creature
That is beloved. How dost thou like this tune?

VIOLA. It gives a very echo to the seat
Where love is throned.

DUKE. Thou dost speak masterly:
My life upon 't, young though thou art, thine eye
Hath stay'd upon some favor that it loves:
Hath it not, boy?

VIOLA. A little, by your favor.

DUKE. What kind of woman is 't?

VIOLA. Of your complexion.

DUKE. She is not worth thee, then. What years, i' faith?

VIOLA. About your years, my lord.

DUKE. Too old, by heaven: let still the woman take
An elder than herself; so wears she to him,
So sways she level in her husband's heart:

5 **airs**: tunes. **recollected terms**: refined words.

6 **giddy-paced**: very quick. **times**: beat, 节拍。

8—9 **He is not here, . . . that / should sing it**: He that should sing it is not here. **so please**: may it please.

14 **the while**: meanwhile.

18 **Unstaid**: unsteady. **skittish**: nervous. **motions else**: other emotions.

19 **Save**: except. **image**: mental picture.

24 **My life upon 't**: I dare stake my life upon it — an oath.

25 **favor**: face.

27 **favor**: leave, permission.

32 **still**: always.

33 **so wears she to him**: so that she may adapt herself to him.

34 **So sways she level**: so that she may hold a steady sway.

For, boy, however we do praise ourselves,
Our fancies are more giddy and unfirm,
More longing, wavering, sooner lost and worn,
Than women's are.

VIOLA. I think it well, my lord.

DUKE. Then let thy love be younger than thyself,
Or thy affection cannot hold the bent;
For women are as roses, whose fair flower
Being once display'd, doth fall that very hour.

VIOLA. And so they are: alas, that they are so;
To die, even when they to perfection grow!

Re-enter CURIO *and* CLOWN.]

DUKE. O, fellow, come, the song we had last night.
Mark it, Cesario, it is old and plain;
The spinsters and the knitters in the sun
And the free maids that weave their thread with bones
Do use to chant it: it is silly sooth,
And dallies with the innocence of love,
Like the old age.

CLOWN. Are you ready, sir?

DUKE. Aye; prithee, sing. [*Music*.

CLOWN. Come away, come away, death,
And in sad cypress let me be laid;
Fly away, fly away, breath;
I am slain by a fair cruel maid.
My shroud of white, stuck all with yew,
O, prepare it!
My part of death, no one so true
Did share it.
Not a flower, not a flower sweet,
On my black coffin let there be strown;
Not a friend, not a friend greet
My poor corpse, where my bones shall be
thrown:

36 **Our fancies**：men's love.

37 **worn**：exhausted.

39 **I think it well**：I think you are right.

41 **Or**：otherwise. **hold the bent**：remain at full stretch（bent 是张满弓）。

43 **display'd**：unfolded，open.

48 **spinsters**：spinners.

49 **free**：free from care.

50 **Do use to chant**：are in the habit of chanting. **silly sooth**：simple truth.

51 **dallies with**：trifles with.

52 **Like the old age**：as in the old days.

55 **Come away**：come hither.

56 **in sad cypress**：① in a coffin of cypress wood；② on a bier strewn with branches of cypress，the dark foliage of which is symbolic of mourning.

60 **it**：指 shroud.

61 **part**：allotted portion.

64 **strown**：strewn.

65 **greet**：bewail.

A thousand thousand sighs to save,
Lay me, O, where
Sad true lover never find my grave,
To weep there!

DUKE. There's for thy pains.

CLOWN. No pains, sir; I take pleasure in singing, sir.

DUKE. I'll pay thy pleasure then.

CLOWN. Truly, sir, and pleasure will be paid, one time or another.

DUKE. Give me now leave to leave thee.

CLOWN. Now, the melancholy god protect thee; and the tailor make thy doublet of changeable taffeta, for thy mind is a very opal. I would have men of such constancy put to sea, that their business might be every thing and their intent every where; for that's it that always makes a good voyage of nothing. Farewell. [*Exit*.

DUKE. Let all the rest give place.
[CURIO *and* ATTENDANTS *retire*.
Once more, Cesario,
Get thee to yond same sovereign cruelty:
Tell her, my love, more noble than the world,
Prizes not quantity of dirty lands;
The parts that fortune hath bestow'd upon her,
Tell her, I hold as giddily as fortune;
But 'tis that miracle and queen of gems
That nature pranks her in attracts my soul.

VIOLA. But if she cannot love you, sir?

DUKE. I cannot be so answer'd.

VIOLA. Sooth, but you must.
Say that some lady, as perhaps there is,
Hath for your love as great a pang of heart
As you have for Olivia: you cannot love her;
You tell her so; must she not then be answer'd?

DUKE. There is no woman's sides

72 **for thy pains**:for your trouble (expression used when giving a tip).

75—76 **will be**: will have to be. **one time or another**:sooner or later. pleasure 开始的这句话是成语。

77 前一个 **leave**:permission,后一个实际等于 dismiss.

78 **melancholy god**:罗马神话中的 Saturn,即土星,主管性格忧郁的人们。

79 **changeable**:varying in color in different lights.

80 **a very opal**:just like an opal (a precious stone in which changes of color are seen). **men of such constancy**:men of little constancy,who often change their minds. 喻没有固定航线的商船的船长。

82 **intent**:aim,bent.

84 **give place**:go away.

86 **Get thee**:you go (imperative mood). **yond**:yonder. **sovereign**:of supreme power,extreme.

87 **more noble than the world**:nobler than anything in the world.

88 **dirty**:of dirt,therefore,not valuable.

89 **parts**:gifts of wealth and position.

90 **hold**:regard. **giddily**:lightly. **fortune**:a fickle goddess.

91 **miracle**:指她的美貌。

92 **pranks**:adorns. **attracts**:前省略 that.

95 **Sooth**:in truth.

96 **Say**:let's say,suppose.

97 **pang of heart**:painful longing.

99 **answer'd**:satisfied.

100 **sides**:chest,body.

Can bide the beating of so strong a passion
As love doth give my heart; no woman's heart
So big, to hold so much; they lack retention.
Alas, their love may be call'd appetite, —
No motion of the liver, but the palate, —
That suffer surfeit, cloyment and revolt;
But mine is all as hungry as the sea,
And can digest as much: make no compare
Between that love a woman can bear me
And that I owe Olivia.

VIOLA. Aye, but I know, —

DUKE. What dost thou know?

VIOLA. Too well what love women to men may owe:
In faith, they are as true of heart as we.
My father had a daughter loved a man,
As it might be, perhaps, were I a woman,
I should your lordship.

DUKE. And what's her history?

VIOLA. A blank, my lord. She never told her love,
But let concealment, like a worm i' the bud,
Feed on her damask cheek; she pined in thought
And with a green and yellow melancholy
She sat like patience on a monument,
Smiling at grief. Was not this love indeed?
We men may say more, swear more: but indeed
Our shows are more than will; for still we prove
Much in our vows, but little in our love.

DUKE. But died thy sister of her love, my boy?

VIOLA. I am all the daughters of my father's house,
And all the brothers too: and yet I know not.
Sir, shall I to this lady?

DUKE. Aye that's the theme.
To her in haste; give her this jewel; say,
My love can give no place, bide no denay. [*Exeunt*.

101 **bide**: bear, endure.

103 **they**: women. **retention**: power to retain (a medical term).

105 **liver**: supposed to be the seat of the passions. **palate**: 腭。

106 **suffer surfeit, cloyment and revolt**: is subjected to fulness, satiety and revulsion.

107 **all**: wholly, completely.

108 **compare**: comparison.

110 **owe**: have for, bear to.

115 **loved**: 前省略 who.

117 **should**: 后省略 love.

119 **told**: revealed.

120 **concealment**: the secret love.

121 **damask**: pink and white like the damask rose.

123 **patience on a monument**: 象征"忍耐"的雕像,是一位女人坐在石上,肩上负轭,脚踩荆棘,多见于王族陵墓旁。

126—127 We display more passion than we actually feel. **still**: always.

132 **theme**: business, matter.

134 **give no place**: make no concession. **bide**: endure. **denay**: denial.

SCENE V

—OLIVIA'S *garden*.

Enter SIR TOBY, SIR ANDREW, *and* FABIAN.]

SIR TOBY. Come thy ways, Signior Fabian.

FABIAN. Nay, I'll come: if I lose a scruple of this sport, let me be boiled to death with melancholy.

SIR TOBY. Wouldst thou not be glad to have the niggardly rascally sheep-biter come by some notable shame?

FABIAN. I would exult, man: you know, he brought me out o' favor with my lady about a bear-baiting here.

SIR TOBY. To anger him we'll have the bear again and we will fool him black and blue: shall we not, Sir Andrew?

SIR ANDREW. An we do not, it is pity of our lives.

SIR TOBY. Here comes the little villain.

Enter MARIA.]

How now, my metal of India!

MARIA. Get ye all three into the box-tree: Malvolio's coming down this walk: he has been yonder i' the sun practising behavior to his own shadow this half hour: observe him, for the love of mockery; for I know this letter will make a contemplative idiot of him. Close, in the name of jesting! Lie thou there [*throws down a letter*]; for here comes the trout that must be caught with tickling. [*Exit*.

Enter MALVOLIO.]

MALVOLIO. 'Tis but fortune; all is fortune. Maria once told me she did affect me: and I have heard herself come thus near, that, should she fancy, it should be one of my complexion. Besides, she uses me with a more exalted respect than any one else that follows her. What should I think on 't?

SIR TOBY. Here's an overweening rogue!

II. v

1 **Come thy ways**: come with us.

2 **Nay**:语气词,这里相当于 sure. **scruple**: little bit.

5 **sheep-biter**:牧羊犬转意 sneaking fellow,这里指 Malvolio.

7 **bear-baiting**:纵狗斗熊的游戏,在伊丽莎白时代很流行,为清教徒所反对。

9 **black and blue**: discolored by bruises(这里系借用)。

10 **An**: if.

12 **metal of India**: gold. metal 和 mettle (勇气)谐音,这里用以嘲笑马伏里奥胆小。

17—18 **Close**: be still. **in the name of jesting!**: for the sake of jesting!

20 **tickling**: flattery. 浅水里的鳟鱼,只要摸到鳃就能捉住。

22 **affect**: to be fond of, love.

23 **come thus near**: say that much. **fancy**: fall in love with anyone.

24 **complexion**: temperament. **uses**: treats.

26 **on 't**: of it.

FABIAN. O, peace! Contemplation makes a rare turkey-cock of him: how he jets under his advanced plumes!

SIR ANDREW. 'Slight, I could so beat the rogue!

SIR TOBY. Peace, I say.

MALVOLIO. To be Count Malvolio!

SIR TOBY. Ah, rogue!

SIR ANDREW. Pistol him, pistol him.

SIR TOBY. Peace, peace!

MALVOLIO. There is example for 't; the lady of the Strachy married the yeoman of the wardrobe.

SIR ANDREW. Fie on him, Jezebel!

FABIAN. O, peace; now he's deeply in: look how imagination blows him.

MALVOLIO. Having been three months married to her, sitting in my state,—

SIR TOBY. O, for a stone-bow, to hit him in the eye!

MALVOLIO. Calling my officers about me, in my branched velvet gown; having come from a day-bed, where I have left Olivia sleeping,—

SIR TOBY. Fire and brimstone!

FABIAN. O, peace, peace!

MALVOLIO. And then to have the humor of state; and after a demure travel of regard, telling them I know my place as I would they should do theirs, to ask for my kinsman Toby, —

SIR TOBY. Bolts and shackles!

FABIAN. O, peace, peace, peace! now, now.

MALVOLIO. Seven of my people, with an obedient start, make out for him: I frown the while; and perchance wind up my watch, or play with my — some rich jewel. Toby approaches; curtsies there to me,—

SIR TOBY. Shall this fellow live?

FABIAN. Though our silence be drawn from us with cars, yet peace.

28—29 **peace!**: silence! **turkey-cock**: 公火鸡。 **jets**: struts. **advanced**: widespread.

30 **'Slight**: by God's light, an oath.

34 **Pistol** (v.): shoot with a pistol.

36 **for 't**: for it.

37 **yeoman of the wardrobe**: 管服饰的侍从。

38 **Fie on him**: expression of disgust. **Jezebel**: 见《圣经·旧约·列王记上》第 17 章 31 节到《列王记下》第 9 章之末，为不得好死的恶妇人。

39 **in**: engaged, involved.

40 **blows**: swells, puffs up.

42 **state**: chair of state. 贵族的上座，上面常有华盖。

43 **stone-bow**: cross-bow for shooting stones.

44—45 **officers**: household servants. **branched velvet**: 织有图案的丝绒。**day-bed**: couch.

47 **Fire and brimstone!**: blast him!

49 **humor**: whim, caprice. **state**: dignified position.

50 **travel of regard**: look around.

51 **would**: wish. **do theirs**: know their places.

53 **Bolts and shackles!**: He should be put under bolts and shackles as a lunatic.

56 **make out for him**: go out to find him.

60 **drawn from us with cars**: 费很大劲才能得到。

MALVOLIO. I extend my hand to him thus, quenching my familiar smile with an austere regard of control,—

SIR TOBY. And does not Toby take you a blow o' the lips then?

MALVOLIO. Saying, 'Cousin Toby, my fortunes having cast me on your niece give me this prerogative of speech,'—

SIR TOBY. What, what?

MALVOLIO. 'You must amend your drunkenness.'

SIR TOBY. Out, scab!

FABIAN. Nay, patience, or we break the sinews of our plot.

MALVOLIO. 'Besides, you waste the treasure of your time with a foolish knight,' —

SIR ANDREW. That's me, I warrant you.

MALVOLIO. 'One Sir Andrew,' —

SIR ANDREW. I knew 'twas I; for many do call me fool.

MALVOLIO. What employment have we here?

[*Taking up the letter*.

FABIAN. Now is the woodcock near the gin.

SIR TOBY. O, peace! and the spirit of humors intimate reading aloud to him.

MALVOLIO. By my life, this is my lady's hand: these be her very C's, her U's, and her T's; and thus makes she her great P's. It is, in contempt of question, her hand.

SIR ANDREW. Her C's, her U's and her T's: why that?

MALVOLIO. [*Reads*] To the unknown beloved, this, and my good wishes: — her very phrases! By your leave, wax. Soft! and the impressure her Lucrece, with which she uses to seal: 'tis my lady. To whom should this be?

FABIAN. This wins him, liver and all.

MALVOLIO. [*Reads*] Jove knows I love:

But who?

Lips, do not move;

62 **quenching**: suppressing.

63 **regard**: look.

64 **take**: strike. **o' the lips**: on the lips.

70 **amend**: correct.

71 **scab**: scurvy fellow.

72 **sinews**: framework.

79 **employment**: business, matter.

80 **gin**: trap.

81—82 后半句: may the genius who guides the capricious prompt him to read the letter aloud.

83 **hand**: handwriting.

85 **in contempt of question**: without doubt.

88 **By your leave, wax**: 对不起，火漆 (sealing wax)——我要启封了。

89 **Soft!**: gently! **impressure**: stamp on the wax. **Lucrece** (Lucretia): 罗马贵夫人鲁克丽丝，贞洁的象征，奥莉维娅的印章上有她的像。

91 **wins**: captures. **liver**: seat of passions. **liver and all**: 是说 He is all excited.

92 **Jove**: 罗马神话中的天神 Jupiter.

No man must know.

'No man must know.' What follows? the numbers altered!

'No man must know:' if this should be thee, Malvolio?

SIR TOBY. Marry, hang thee, brock!

MALVOLIO. [*Reads*] I may command where I adore;
But silence, like a Lucrece knife,
With bloodless stroke my heart doth gore:
M, O, A, I, doth sway my life.

FABIAN. A fustian riddle!

SIR TOBY. Excellent wench, say I.

MALVOLIO. 'M, O, A, I, doth sway my life.' Nay, but first, let me see, let me see, let me see.

FABIAN. What dish o' poison has she dressed him!

SIR TOBY. And with what wing the staniel checks at it!

MALVOLIO. 'I may command where I adore.' Why, she may command me: I serve her; she is my lady. Why, this is evident to any formal capacity; there is no obstruction in this: and the end, — what should that alphabetical position portend? If I could make that resemble something in me, — Softly! M, O, A, I, —

SIR TOBY. O, aye, make up that: he is now at a cold scent.

FABIAN. Sowter will cry upon 't for all this, though it be as rank as a fox.

MALVOLIO. M, — Malvolio; M, — why, that begins my name.

FABIAN. Did not I say he would work it out? the cur is excellent at faults.

MALVOLLO. M, — but then there is no consonancy in the sequel; that suffers under probation: A should follow, but O does.

FABIAN. And O shall end, I hope.

SIR TOBY. Aye, or I'll cudgel him, and make him cry O!

MALVOLIO. And then I comes behind.

96 numbers：meter，诗的韵律。

99 brock：badger，獾。这是说他像獾一样在挖掘（信中的秘密）。

101 a Lucrece knife：Lucrece's knife. 鲁克丽丝在被奸污后自杀，参见莎士比亚《鲁克丽丝受辱记》。

102 gore：pierce.

104 fustian：ridiculously pompous.

105 Excellent wench：赞 Maria 编造得好。

108 dressed him：prepared for him.

109 staniel：inferior kind of hawk. **checks at it**：swerves to pounce on it.

112—113 any formal capacity：anyone of a well-regulated mind. **obstruction**：difficulty.

114 position：arrangement. **portend**：mean.

116 make up that：try hard. **at a cold scent**：(like a hound) picking up a wrong scent weakened by passage of time.

117 Sowter：cobbler，name of a poor hound. **cry upon 't**：yelp at the scent.

118 rank：of offensively strong smell.

122 faults：breaks in the line of scent.

123 consonancy：consistency.

124 probation：trial，investigation.

FABIAN. Aye, an you had any eye behind you, you might see more detraction at your heels than fortunes before you.

MALVOLIO. M, O, A, I; this simulation is not as the former: and yet, to crush this a little, it would bow to me, for every one of these letters are in my name. Soft! here follows prose.

[*Reads*] If this fall into thy hand, revolve. In my stars I am above thee; but be not afraid of greatness: some are born great, some achieve greatness, and some have greatness thrust upon 'em. Thy Fates open their hands; let thy blood and spirit embrace them; and, to inure thyself to what thou art like to be, cast thy humble slough and appear fresh. Be opposite with a kinsman, surly with servants; let thy tongue tang arguments of state; put thyself into the trick of singularity: she thus advises thee that sighs for thee. Remember who commended thy yellow stockings, and wished to see thee ever cross-gartered: I say, remember. Go to, thou art made, if thou desirest to be so; if not, let me see thee a steward still, the fellow of servants, and not worthy to touch Fortune's fingers. Farewell. She that would alter services with thee,

THE FORTUNATE-UNHAPPY.

Daylight and champaign discovers not more; this is open. I will be proud, I will read politic authors, I will baffle Sir Toby, I will wash off gross acquaintance, I will be point-devise the very man. I do not now fool myself, to let imagination jade me; for every reason excites to this, that my lady loves me. She did commend my yellow stockings of late, she did praise my leg being cross-gartered; and in this she manifests herself to my love, and with a kind of injunction drives me to these habits of her liking. I thank my stars I am happy. I will

129 **an**: if.

130 **detraction**: lessening of reputation or esteem.

132—133 **simulation**: riddle. **the former**: 指'I may command where I adore'. **crush**: break. **bow**: yield.

136 **revolve**: consider. **stars**: fortune.

140 **inure**: get used, habituate.

141 **art like to be**: can reasonably expect to be.

142 **slough**: old skin (as of a snake). **opposite with**: hostile towards.

143 **tang**: sound loud with.

144 **trick of singularity**: affectation of eccentricity.

146 **yellow stockings**: ①奥莉维娅不喜欢黄色;②黄色长筒袜早已过时;③家中居丧,黄色也不相宜。

147 **cross-gartered**: 吊袜带在膝后弯处交叉,在膝盖上前方系结,这种系带法也已过时。 **Go to**: come now(语气词)。

148 **made**: ensured success in life.

153 **champaign**: flat open country. **discovers**: reveals.

155 **baffle**: disgrace. **wash off**: get rid of.

156 **point-devise**: to the last detail.

157—158 **jade**: deceive. **excites to this**: encourages me to believe in this.

160—161 **manifests herself to my love**: makes known her love for me. **drives me**: urges me on.

162 **habits**: clothes.

be strange, stout, in yellow stockings, and cross-gartered, even with the swiftness of putting on. Jove and my stars be praised! Here is yet a postscript. [*Reads*] Thou canst not choose but know who I am. If thou entertainest my love, let it appear in thy smiling; thy smiles become thee well; therefore in my presence still smile, dear my sweet, I prithee.

Jove, I thank thee: I will smile; I will do everything that thou wilt have me. [*Exit*.

FABIAN. I will not give my part of this sport for a pension of thousands to be paid from the Sophy.

SIR TOBY. I could marry this wench for this device,—

SIR ANDREW. So could I too.

SIR TOBY. And ask no other dowry with her but such another jest.

SIR ANDREW. Nor I neither.

FABIAN. Here comes my noble gull-catcher.

Re-enter MARIA.]

SIR TOBY. Wilt thou set thy foot o' my neck?

SIR ANDREW. Or o' mine either?

SIR TOBY. Shall I play my freedom at tray-trip, and become thy bond-slave?

SIR ANDREW. I' faith, or I either?

SIR TOBY. Why, thou hast put him in such a dream, that when the image of it leaves him he must run mad.

MARIA. Nay, but say true; does it work upon him?

SIR TOBY. Like aqua-vitæ with a midwife.

MARIA. If you will then see the fruits of the sport, mark his first approach before my lady: he will come to her in yellow stockings, and 'tis a color she abhors, and cross-gartered, a fashion she detests; and he will smile upon her, which will now be so unsuitable to her disposition, being addicted to a melancholy as she is, that cannot but turn him into a notable contempt. If you will

163 **strange**：aloof. **stout**：proud，haughty.

167 **entertainest**：take pleasure in，accept（-est 为第二人称谓语动词的形变）。

169 **still**：always.

170 **Jove**：by Jove（发誓语）。

171 **thou wilt have me**：you will have me do.

173 **Sophy**：Shah of Persia. 1600 年伦敦有小册子报道英国冒险家观察到的波斯王宫廷的情况。

179 **gull-catcher**：trickster.

180 我对你佩服得五体投地了（愿让你的脚踩在我脖子上）。

182 **tray-trip**：game at dice，success in which depends on throwing a three，掷骰戏，以掷得三点取胜。

186 **run mad**：go mad.

187 **say true**：tell me the truth.

188 **aqua-vitæ**：alcoholic spirits，烧酒。

195 **notable contempt**：infamous disgrace.

see it, follow me.

SIR TOBY. To the gates of Tartar, thou most excellent devil of wit!

SIR ANDREW. I'll make one too. [*Exeunt*.

197 **Tartar**：Tartarus，希神罗神话中地狱的底层。

ACT III

SCENE I

—OLIVIA'S *garden*.

Enter VIOLA, *and* CLOWN *with a tabor*.]

VIOLA. Save thee, friend, and thy music: dost thou live by thy tabor?

CLOWN. No, sir, I live by the church.

VIOLA. Art thou a churchman?

CLOWN. No such matter, sir: I do live by the church; for I do live at my house, and my house doth stand by the church.

VIOLA. So thou mayst say, the king lies by a beggar, if a beggar dwell near him; or, the church stands by thy tabor, if thy tabor stand by the church.

CLOWN. You have said, sir. To see this age! A sentence is but a cheveril glove to a good wit: how quickly the wrong side may be turned outward!

VIOLA. Nay, that's certain; they that dally nicely with words may quickly make them wanton.

CLOWN. I would, therefore, my sister had had no name, sir.

VIOLA. Why, man?

CLOWN. Why, sir, her name's a word; and to dally with that word might make my sister wanton. But indeed words are very rascals since bonds disgraced them.

VIOLA. Thy reason, man?

CLOWN. Troth, sir, I can yield you none without words; and words are grown so false, I am loath to prove reason with them.

III. i

1 **Save thee**：short for ‘God save thee’，上帝保佑你。

2 **tabor**：small drum.

3 **live by**：①live near；②live on，靠某事过活。

8 **lies by**：①dwells near；②sleeps with.

9 **stands by**：①stands near；②is upheld by.

11 **You have said**：you have spoken to the point，你说得对。 **To see**：look at.

12 **cheveril**：kid-leather，小山羊皮。

14 **dally**：trifle，play subtly.

15 **wanton**：①equivocal；②unchaste.

16 **would**：wish.

21 **bonds**：linkage. **disgraced**：disfigure.

23 **Troth**：by my troth，说真的。 **can yield you none**：cannot give you any reason.

24 **are grown**：have become.

VIOLA. I warrant thou art a merry fellow and carest for nothing.

CLOWN. Not so, sir, I do care for something; but in my conscience, sir, I do not care for you: if that be to care for nothing, sir, I would it would make you invisible.

VIOLA. Art not thou the Lady Olivia's fool?

CLOWN. No, indeed, sir! the Lady Olivia has no folly: she will keep no fool, sir, till she be married; and fools are as like husbands as pilchards are to herrings; the husband's the bigger: I am indeed not her fool, but her corrupter of words.

VIOLA. I saw thee late at the Count Orsino's.

CLOWN. Foolery, sir does walk about the orb like the sun, it shines every where. I would be sorry, sir, but the fool should be as oft with your master as with my mistress: I think I saw your wisdom there.

VIOLA. Nay, an thou pass upon me, I'll no more with thee. Hold, there's expenses for thee.

CLOWN. Now Jove, in his next commodity of hair, send thee a beard!

VIOLA. By my troth, I'll tell thee, I am almost sick for one; [*Aside*] though I would not have it grow on my chin. Is thy lady within?

CLOWN. Would not a pair of these have bred, sir?

VIOLA. Yes, being kept together and put to use.

CLOWN. I would play Lord Pandarus of Phrygia, sir, to bring a Cressida to this Troilus.

VIOLA. I understand you, sir; 'tis well begged.

CLOWN. The matter, I hope, is not great, sir, begging but a beggar: Cressida was a beggar. My lady is within, sir. I will construe to them whence you come; who you are and what you would are out of my welkin, I might say 'element,' but the word is overworn. [*Exit*.

VIOLA. This fellow is wise enough to play the fool;

26 I warrant:I dare say.

28—29 care for:①be worried about;②feel concern for;③have a liking for,多义文字游戏。**in my conscience**:upon my conscience,凭良心说。

37 late:not long ago.

41 your wisdom:①an ironic courtesy title;②你这位聪明人;③你的智慧。

42 an:if. **pass upon**:jest at.

43 expenses:赏钱。

44 commodity:consignment. 他注意到女扮男装的薇奥拉无胡须。

46 By my troth:in faith. **sick for**:long for.

47 one:a beard,胡子。

49 these:coins. **have bred**:have produced offspring.

51 Pandarus:中世纪故事中把 Cressida 和 Troilus 拉在一起的媒人,乔叟和莎士比亚都有关于这个故事的著作。Henryson 的诗 *The Testament of Cresseid* (1593)中写到 Cressida 后来成为乞丐。

56 construe:explain.

57 welkin:sphere.

And to do that well craves a kind of wit:
He must observe their mood on whom he jests,
The quality of persons, and the time,
And, like the haggard, check at every feather
That comes before his eye. This is a practice
As full of labor as a wise man's art:
For folly that he wisely shows is fit;
But wise men, folly-fall'n, quite taint their wit.

Enter SIR TOBY, *and* SIR ANDREW.]

SIR TOBY. Save you, gentleman.

VIOLA. And you, sir.

SIR ANDREW. Dieu vous garde, monsieur.

VIOLA. Et vous aussi; votre serviteur.

SIR ANDREW. I hope, sir, you are; and I am yours.

SIR TOBY. Will you encounter the house? my niece is desirous you should enter, if your trade be to her.

VIOLA. I am bound to your niece, sir; I mean, she is the list of my voyage.

SIR TOBY. Taste your legs, sir; put them to motion.

VIOLA. My legs do better understand me, sir, than I understand what you mean by bidding me taste my legs.

SIR TOBY. I mean, to go, sir, to enter.

VIOLA. I will answer you with gait and entrance. But we are prevented.

Enter OLIVIA *and* MARIA.]

Most excellent accomplished lady, the heavens rain odors on you!

SIR ANDREW. That youth's a rare courtier: 'Rain odors;' well.

VIOLA. My matter hath no voice, lady, but to your own most pregnant and vouchsafed ear.

SIR ANDREW. 'Odors,' 'pregnant,' and 'vouchsafed:' I'll get 'em all three all ready.

OLIVIA. Let the garden door be shut, and leave me to my

60 **craves**: requires.

63 **haggard**: wild hawk. **check at**: swoop on. **feather**: bird.

64 **his**: its.

66 **fit**: to the point.

67 **folly-fall'n**: lapsed into folly. **taint**: stain, impair.

68 **Save you**: God save you.

70 **Dieu vous garde, monsieur** 〈法语〉: God keep you, sir.

71 **Et vous aussi; votre serviteur**〈法语〉: And you too; (I am) your servant.

73 **encounter**: approach（一种做作的说法）。

74 **trade**: business.

76 **list**: objective.

77 **Taste**: try out.

82 **prevented**: forestalled.

84 **odors**: perfume.

87 **matter**: business.

88 **pregnant**: receptive. **vouchsafed**: condescending, attentive.

hearing. [*Exeunt* SIR TOBY, SIR ANDREW, *and* MARIA.]
Give me your hand, sir.

VIOLA. My duty, madam, and most humble service.

OLIVIA. What is your name?

VIOLA. Cesario is your servant's name, fair princess.

OLIVIA. My servant, sir! 'Twas never merry world
Since lowly feigning was call'd compliment:
You're servant to the Count Orsino, youth.

VIOLA. And he is yours, and his must needs be yours:
Your servant's servant is your servant, madam.

OLIVIA. For him, I think not on him: for his thoughts,
Would they were blanks, rather than fill'd with me!

VIOLA. Madam, I come to whet your gentle thoughts
On his behalf.

OLIVIA. O, by your leave, I pray you;
I bade you never speak again of him:
But, would you undertake another suit,
I had rather hear you to solicit that
Than music from the spheres.

VIOLA. Dear lady, —

OLIVIA. Give me leave, beseech you. I did send,
After the last enchantment you did here,
A ring in chase of you: so did I abuse
Myself, my servant and, I fear me, you:
Under your hard construction must I sit,
To force that on you, in a shameful cunning,
Which you knew none of yours: what might you think?
Have you not set mine honor at the stake
And baited it with all the unmuzzled thoughts
That tyrannous heart can think? To one of your receiving
Enough is shown; a cypress, not a bosom,
Hides my heart. So, let me hear you speak.

VIOLA. I pity you.

92 **hearing**:interview.

97 **'Twas never merry world**:(a catchphrase) things have never been the same.

98 **lowly feigning**:affected humbleness.

102 **For**:as for. **on**:of.

103 **Would**:I wish.

104 **whet**:incite.

108 **would you**:if you should.

110 **music from the spheres**:古代天文学认为天是由几层水晶球套成,转动时摩擦,产生音乐。

112 **beseech**:前省略 I.

114 **abuse**:cheat.

115 **I fear me**:I am afraid (me 在这里是语助词)。

116 **hard**:harsh. **construction**:judgement.

118 **none**:前省略 to be.

119—120 这里借用纵犬斗熊游戏的比喻。**stake**:拴熊的柱子。**baited**:纵物去咬。**unmuzzled**:去掉嘴罩的。**thoughts**:喻狗。

121 **tyrannous**:pitiless,cruel.

122 **receiving**:perception.

123 **cypress**:black mourning scarf.

OLIVIA. That's a degree to love.
VIOLA. No, not a grize; for 'tis a vulgar proof,
That very oft we pity enemies.
OLIVIA. Why, then, methinks 'tis time to smile again.
O world, how apt the poor are to be proud!
If one should be a prey, how much the better
To fall before the lion than the wolf! [*Clock strikes*.
The clock upbraids me with the waste of time.
Be not afraid, good youth, I will not have you:
And yet, when wit and youth is come to harvest,
Your wife is like to reap a proper man;
There lies your way, due west.
VIOLA Then westward-ho!
Grace and good disposition attend your ladyship!
You'll nothing, madam, to my lord by me?
OLIVIA. Stay:
I prithee, tell me what thou think'st of me.
VIOLA. That you do think you are not what you are.
OLIVIA. If I think so, I think the same of you.
VIOLA. Then think you right: I am not what I am.
OLIVIA. I would you were as I would have you be!
VIOLA. Would it be better, madam, than I am?
I wish it might, for now I am your fool.
OLIVIA. O, what a deal of scorn looks beautiful
In the contempt and anger of his lip!
A murderous guilt shows not itself more soon
Than love that would seem hid: love's night is noon.
Cesario, by the roses of the spring,
By maidhood, honor, truth and every thing,
I love thee so, that, mauger all thy pride,
Nor wit nor reason can my passion hide.
Do not extort thy reasons from this clause,
For that I woo, thou therefore hast no cause;
But rather reason thus with reason fetter,

126 **degree**: step.

127 **grize**: step. **vulgar proof**: common experience.

134 **have**: hold, detain.

136 **like**: likely. **proper**: handsome.

138 **westward-ho**: 当时泰晤士河上的船夫常呼 westward-ho 或 eastward-ho，以免船只相撞。

143 You forget yourself.

144 后半句 I too think you are not what you appear to be.

149 **deal**: considerable amount. 注意从这行起改用两行一韵脚，表示诗情的提高。

152 **hid**: hidden. **love's night is noon**: love's secret is apparent.

154 **maidhood**: maidenhood.

155 **thee**: 注意 Olivia 前面一直称 Cesario 为 you，因他是低一等的人；这里却情不自禁，换了爱称的 thee. **mauger**(来自法语 malgré): in spite of.

156 **wit**: common sense.

157 Do not infer from my declaration the idea that....

158 Because I woo you, you have no cause to love me.

159 But rather govern this idea with the reasoning that....

Love sought is good, but given unsought is better.

VIOLA. By innocence I swear, and by my youth,
I have one heart, one bosom and one truth,
And that no woman has; nor never none
Shall mistress be of it, save I alone.
And so adieu, good madam: never more
Will I my master's tears to you deplore.

OLIVIA. Yet come again; for thou perhaps mayst move
That heart, which now abhors, to like his love.

[*Exeunt*.

SCENE II

—OLIVIA'S *house*.

Enter SIR TOBY, SIR ANDREW, *and* FABIAN.]

SIR ANDREW. No, faith, I'll not stay a jot longer.

SIR TOBY. Thy reason, dear venom, give thy reason.

FABIAN. You must needs yield your reason, Sir Andrew.

SIR ANDREW. Marry, I saw your niece do more favors to the count's serving-man than ever she bestowed upon me; I saw 't i' the orchard.

SIR TOBY. Did she see thee the while, old boy? tell me that.

SIR ANDREW. As plain as I see you now.

FABIAN. This was a great argument of love in her toward you.

SIR ANDREW. 'Slight, will you make an ass o' me?

FABIAN. I will prove it legitimate, sir, upon the oaths of judgment and reason.

SIR TOBY. And they have been grand-jurymen since before Noah was a sailor.

FABIAN. She did show favor to the youth in your sight only to exasperate you, to awake your dormouse valor, to put fire in your heart, and brimstone in your liver. You should then have accosted her; and with some

166 **deplore**:tell with grief.

168 **That**:the.

III. ii

3 **yield**:give.

7 **the while**:at that time.

9 **argument**:proof.

11 **'Slight**:by God's light.

12 **legitimate**:logically inferred.

14 **they**:指 judgement and reason.

15 **Noah**:诺亚。传说中古时按神示驾方舟逃脱洪水灾害的人,见《圣经·旧约·创世记》第6到8章。

17 **dormouse**:睡鼠。此处假借为 dormant,timid (adj.).

excellent jests, fire-new from the mint, you should have banged the youth into dumbness. This was looked for at your hand, and this was balked: the double gilt of this opportunity you let time wash off, and you are now sailed into the north of my lady's opinion; where you will hang like an icicle on a Dutchman's beard, unless you do redeem it by some laudable attempt either of valor or policy.

SIR ANDREW. An 't be any way, it must be with valor; for policy I hate: I had as lief be a Brownist as a politician.

SIR TOBY. Why, then, build me thy fortunes upon the basis of valor. Challenge me the count's youth to fight with him; hurt him in eleven places: my niece shall take note of it; and assure thyself, there is no love-broker in the world can more prevail in man's commendation with woman than report of valor.

FABIAN. There is no way but this, Sir Andrew.

SIR ANDREW. Will either of you bear me a challenge to him?

SIR TOBY. Go, write it in a martial hand; be curst and brief; it is no matter how witty, so it be eloquent and full of invention: taunt him with the license of ink: if thou thou 'st him some thrice, it shall not be amiss; and as many lies as will lie in thy sheet of paper, although the sheet were big enough for the bed of Ware in England, set 'em down: go, about it. Let there be gall enough in thy ink, though thou write with a goose-pen, no matter: about it.

SIR ANDREW. Where shall I find you?

SIR TOBY. We'll call thee at the cubiculo: go.

[*Exit* SIR ANDREW.

FABIAN. This is a dear manakin to you, Sir Toby.

SIR TOBY. I have been dear to him, lad, some two thousand strong, or so.

20 **fire-new**: brand-new.

21—22 **banged**: knocked. **looked for at your hand**: expected of you.

22 **balked**: shirked. **double gilt**: brightness of a twice-gilded gold plate.

24 **north**: cold.

25 可能暗指荷兰航海家 Willem Barentsz 的北极探险(1596—1597)。

27 **policy**: tact, stratagem.

28 **An**: if.

29 **lief**: gladly. **Brownist**: 当时英国清教徒 Robert Brown 为首的一种教派的成员。**politician**: schemer.

30 **build me thy fortunes**: 和下一行的 Challenge me the count's youth 相同,这里的 me 都是语助词,带有 on my advice 的意味。

33 **love-broker**: go-between.

34—35 **can**: 前省略 that. **prevail in man's commendation with woman**: promote a man in a woman's favor.

37 **bear me**: convey for me.

39 **curst**: petulant.

40 **so it be**: so long as it is.

41 **with the license of ink**: with things you dare not say to his face. **license**: freedom of action.

42 **thou'st him**: address him as 'thou' ('thou' is sometimes used in contemptuous or angry speech).

43 **lie**: ①(n.)谎言;②(v.)躺。**sheet**: ①纸张;②床单。

44 **bed of Ware**: 有名的伊丽莎白时代大床,长宽各近 11 英尺,可睡 12 人,现在伦敦"维多利亚和艾伯特博物馆"。

45 **about it**: get to work. **gall**: bitterness.

46—47 **goose-pen**: symbolic of cowardice. **though ... / no matter**: it doesn't matter if.

49 **cubiculo** 〈意大利语〉: small partitioned place for private discussion.

50 **manakin**: manikin, dwarf, puppet.

51 **dear**: expensive.

52 **strong**: in number (of pounds).

FABIAN. We shall have a rare letter from him: but you 'll not deliver 't?

SIR TOBY. Never trust me, then; and by all means stir on the youth to an answer. I think oxen and wainropes cannot hale them together. For Andrew, if he were opened, and you find so much blood in his liver as will clog the foot of a flea, I'll eat the rest of the anatomy.

FABIAN. And his opposite, the youth, bears in his visage no great presage of cruelty.

Enter MARIA.]

SIR TOBY. Look, where the youngest wren of nine comes.

MARIA. If you desire the spleen, ad will laugh yourselves into stitches, follow me. Yond gull Malvolio is turned heathen, a very renegado; for there is no Christian, that means to be saved by believing rightly, can ever believe such impossible passages of grossness. He 's in yellow stockings.

SIR TOBY. And cross-gartered?

MARIA. Most villainously; like a pedant that keeps a school i' the church. I have dogged him, like his murderer. He does obey every point of the letter that I dropped to betray him: he does smile his face into more lines than is in the new map with the augmentation of the Indies: you have not seen such thing as 'tis. I can hardly forbear hurling things at him. I know my lady will strike him: if she do, he 'll smile and take 't for a great favor.

SIR TOBY. Come, bring us, bring us where he is. [*Exeunt*.

SCENE III

—A street.

Enter SEBASTIAN *and* ANTONIO.]

SEBASTIAN. I would not by my will have troubled you;

55 **stir on**: incite.

56 **wainropes**: waggon-ropes.

57—58 **hale**: haul, pull. **For**: as for. **if he were opened**: if his body were cut open.

59 **anatomy**: body.

61 **presage**: omen, sign.

62 **youngest wren of nine**:鹪鹩产九蛋,最后孵出的鸟最小。

63 **spleen**: fit of laughter.

64 **stitches**: fits of pain in side of body.

65 **renegado**: renegade.

67 **passages**: statements (in Maria's letter). **grossness**: stupidity.

70 **pedant that ...** :旧时有些教师在教堂教学生,无另外的校舍。

74 **new map...** :1599 年出版 Emmeric Mollineux 画的世界地图,上有许多恒向线,并第一次标出了东印度群岛。

III. iii

1 **troubled you**: to follow me to the city.

But, since you make your pleasure of your pains, I will no further chide you.

ANTONIO. I could not stay behind you; my desire,
More sharp than filed steel, did spur me forth;
And not all love to see you, though so much
As might have drawn one to a longer voyage,
But jealousy what might befall your travel,
Being skilless in these parts; which to a stranger,
Unguided and unfriended, often prove
Rough and unhospitable: my willing love
The rather by these arguments of fear,
Set forth in your pursuit.

SEBASTIAN. My kind Antonio,
I can no other answer make but thanks.
And thanks; and ever thanks; and oft good turns
Are shuffled off with such uncurrent pay:
But, were my worth as is my conscience firm,
You should find better dealing. What 's to do?
Shall we go see the reliques of this town?

ANTONIO. To-morrow, sir: best first go see your lodging.

SEBASTIAN. I am not weary, and 'tis long to night:
I pray you, let us satisfy our eyes
With the memorials and the things of fame
That do renown this city.

ANTONIO. Would you 'ld pardon me;
I do not without danger walk these streets:
Once, in a sea-fight, 'gainst the count his galleys
I did some service; of such note indeed,
That were I ta'en here it would scarce be answer'd.

SEBASTIAN. Belike you slew great number of his people.

ANTONIO. The offense is not of such a bloody nature;
Albeit the quality of the time and quarrel
Might well have given us bloody argument.
It might have since been answer'd in repaying

4 **behind you**: behind.

5 **filed**: sharpened with a file.

6 **not all**: not only.

8 **jealousy**: apprehension, concern.

9 **Being**:前省略 you. **skilless in**: unacquainted with.

12 **rather**: more speedily. **by**: as a consequence of. **arguments**: reasons.

13 **Set forth**: set me forth.

16 **oft**: often. **turns**: services.

17 **shuffled off**: paid off. **uncurrent**: out of currency, worthless.

18 **worth**: wealth, means. **conscience**: awareness of my debt to you. **firm**: certain.

19 **You should find better dealing**: you would be better paid.

20 **reliques**: antiquities, sights.

22 **long to night**: much time before nightfall.

25 **renown**: make famous.

26 **Would you 'ld**: I wish you would.

28 **'gainst the count his galleys**: against the count's galleys.

29 **note**: attention.

30 **ta'en**: taken, seized. **it would scarce be answer'd**: it could hardly be remedied.

31 **Belike**: perhaps. **great**:前省略 a.

33 **Albeit**: although. **quality**: character.

34 **given us bloody argument**: justified bloodshed.

What we took from them; which, for traffic's sake,
Most of our city did: only myself stood out;
For which, if I be lapsèd in this place,
I shall pay dear.

SEBASTIAN. Do not then walk too open.

ANTONIO. It doth not fit me. Hold, sir, here 's my purse.
In the south suburbs, at the Elephant,
Is best to lodge: I will bespeak our diet,
Whiles you beguile the time and feed your knowledge
With viewing of the town: there shall you have me.

SEBASTIAN. Why I your purse?

ANTONIO. Haply your eye shall light upon some toy
You have desire to purchase; and your store,
I think, is not for idle markets, sir.

SEBASTIAN. I'll be your purse-bearer and leave you
For an hour.

ANTONIO. To the Elephant.

SEBASTIAN. I do remember. [*Exeunt*.

SCENE IV

—OLIVIA'S *garden*.

Enter OLIVIA *and* MARIA.]

OLIVIA. I have sent after him: he says he 'll come;
How shall I feast him? what bestow of him?
For youth is bought more oft than begg'd or borrow'd.
I speak too loud.
Where is Malvolio? he is sad and civil,
And suits well for a servant with my fortunes:
Where is Malvolio?

MARIA. He 's coming, madam; but in very strange manner. He is, sure, possessed, madam.

OLIVIA. Why, what's the matter? does he rave?

MARIA. No, madam, he does nothing but smile: your

36 **traffic's**:trade's.

37 **stood out**:failed to repay.

38 **lapsèd**:captured.

42 **Elephant**:当时在泰晤士河南岸"寰球剧院"附近,有一家旅店叫 The Elephant.

43 **bespeak**:order. **diet**:food,fare.

44 **Whiles**:while. **beguile**:while away. **feed**:enrich.

45 **there**:at the Elephant. **have**:find.

46 **Why I your purse**?:Why should I keep your purse?

47 **Haply**:perhaps.

48 **store**:money.

49 **idle markets**:unnecessary purchase.

III. iv

1 **he says he 'll come**:supposing he says he will come.

2 **bestow of**:(shall I) give.

5 **sad and civil**:grave and sedate.

6 is very suitable as my servant when I am in my present condition (为哥哥居丧)。

9 **possessed**:by a devil.

ladyship were best to have some guard about you, if he come; for, sure, the man is tainted in 's wits.

OLIVIA. Go call him hither. [*Exit* MARIA.] I am as mad as he, If sad and merry madness equal be.

Re-enter MARIA, *with* MALVOLIO.]

How now, Malvolio!

MALVOLIO. Sweet lady, ho, ho.

OLIVIA. Smilest thou?
I sent for thee upon a sad occasion.

MALVOLIO. Sad, lady? I could be sad: this does make some obstruction in the blood, this cross-gartering; but what of that? if it please the eye of one, it is with me as the very true sonnet is, 'Please one, and please all.'

OLIVIA. Why, how dost thou, man? what is the matter with thee?

MALVOLIO. Not black in my mind, though yellow in my legs. It did come to his hands, and commands shall be executed: I think we do know the sweet Roman hand.

OLIVIA. Wilt thou go to bed, Malvolio?

MALVOLIO. To bed! aye, sweet-heart, and I 'll come to thee.

OLIVIA. God comfort thee! Why dost thou smile so and kiss thy hand so oft?

MARIA. How do you, Malvolio?

MALVOLIO. At your request! yes; nightingales answer daws.

MARIA. Why appear you with this ridiculous boldness before my lady?

MALVOLIO. 'Be not afraid of greatness:' 'twas well writ.

OLIVIA. What meanest thou by that, Malvolio?

MALVOLIO. 'Some are born great,' —

OLIVIA. Ha!

MALVOLIO. 'Some achieve greatness,' —

13 **tainted in 's wits**: injured in his wits.

23 **sonnet**: song.

25 **black**: melancholy.

26 **It**: the letter.

28—29 **Roman hand**:意大利式斜体书法。

31 从 aye 开始,为一首流行歌曲的歌词。

37 **daws**: jackdaws,寒鸦。

OLIVIA. What sayest thou?

MALVOLIO. 'And some have greatness thrust upon them.'

OLIVIA. Heaven restore thee!

MALVOLIO. 'Remember who commended thy yellow stockings,' —

OLIVIA. Thy yellow stockings!

MALVOLIO. 'And wished to see thee cross-gartered.'

OLIVIA. Cross-gartered!

MALVOLIO. 'Go to, thou art made, if thou desirest to be so;' —

OLIVIA. Am I made?

MALVOLIO. 'If not, let me see thee a servant still.'

OLIVIA. Why, this is very midsummer madness.

Enter SERVANT.]

SERVANT. Madam, the young gentleman of the Count Orsino's is returned: I could hardly entreat him back: he attends your ladyship's pleasure.

OLIVIA. I'll come to him. [*Exit* SERVANT.] Good Maria, let this fellow be looked to. Where 's my cousin Toby? Let some of my people have a special care of him: I would not have him miscarry for the half of my dowry.

[*Exeunt* OLIVIA *and* MARIA.

MALVOLIO. O. ho! do you come near me now? no worse man than Sir Toby to look to me! This concurs directly with the letter: she sends him on purpose, that I may appear stubborn to him: for she incites me to that in the letter. 'Cast thy humble slough,' says she; 'be opposite with a kinsman, surly with servants; let thy tongue tang with arguments of state; put thyself into the trick of singularity;' and consequently sets down the manner how; as, a sad face, a reverend carriage, a slow tongue, in the habit of some sir of note, and so forth. I have limed her; but it is Jove's doing, and Jove make me thankful! And when she went away

57 **midsummer madness**：当时迷信暑热能使狗发疯。

59 **is returned**：has come back.

62 **be looked to**：be looked after.

64 **miscarry**：come to harm.

65 **come near**：understand.

66 **directly**：exactly，precisely.

72 **consequently**：subsequently，afterwards.

74 **sir**：gentleman，personage. **note**：distinction，importance.

75 **limed**：caught（with birdlime）.

now, 'Let this fellow be looked to:' fellow! not Malvolio, nor after my degree, but fellow. Why, every thing adheres together, that no dram of a scruple, no scruple of a scruple, no obstacle, no incredulous or unsafe circumstance — What can be said? Nothing that can be can come between me and the full prospect of my hopes. Well, Jove, not I, is the doer of this, and he is to be thanked.

Re-enter MARIA, *with* SIR TOBY *and* FABIAN.]

SIR TOBY. Which way is he, in the name of sanctity? If all the devils of hell be drawn in little, and Legion himself possessed him, yet I'll speak to him.

FABIAN. Here he is, here he is. How is 't with you, sir? how is 't with you, man?

MALVOLIO. Go off; I discard you: let me enjoy my private: go off.

MARIA. Lo, how hollow the fiend speaks within him! did not I tell you? Sir Toby, my lady prays you to have a care of him.

MALVOLIO. Ah, ha! does she so?

SIR TOBY. Go to, go to; peace, peace; we must deal gently with him; let me alone. How do you, Malvolio? how is 't with you? What, man! defy the devil: consider, he 's an enemy to mankind.

MALVOLIO. Do you know what you say?

MARIA. La you, an you speak ill of the devil, how he takes it at heart! Pray God, he be not bewitched!

FABIAN. Carry his water to the wise woman.

MARIA. Marry, and it shall be done to-morrow morning, if I live. My lady would not lose him for more than I'll say.

MALVOLIO. How now, mistress!

MARIA. O Lord!

SIR TOBY. Prithee, hold thy peace; this is not the way: do

78 **after**：according to. **degree**：status. **fellow**：①家伙；②同伴。

79 **adheres together**：hangs together. **that**：that there can be. **dram**：very small quantity. **scruple**：①doubt；②minute quantity.

80 **incredulous**：incredible.

86 **drawn in little**：contracted to minute size. **Legion**：（集合名词）host of devils，见《圣经·新约·马可福音》第5章9节。

90 **discard**：dismiss. **private**：privacy.

97 **let me alone**：let me deal with this.

101—102 **La you**：look you. **an**：if. **takes it at heart**：will take it to heart.

102 **he be not bewitched!**：don't let him be bewitched!

103 **water**：urine. **wise woman**：woman skilled in occult arts, witch.

107 **mistress**：miss.

you not see you move him? let me alone with him.

FABIAN. No way but gentleness; gently, gently: the fiend is rough, and will not be roughly used.

SIR TOBY. Why, how now, my bawcock! how dost thou, chuck?

MALVOLIO. Sir!

SIR TOBY. Aye, Biddy, come with me. What, man! 'tis not for gravity to play at cherry-pit with Satan: hang him, foul collier!

MARIA. Get him to say his prayers, good Sir Toby, get him to pray.

MALVOLIO. My prayers, minx!

MARIA. No, I warrant you, he will not hear of godliness.

MALVOLIO. Go, hang yourselves all! you are idle shallow things: I am not of your element: you shall know more hereafter. [*Exit*.

SIR TOBY. Is 't possible?

FABIAN. If this were played upon a stage now, I could condemn it as an improbable fiction.

SIR TOBY. His very genius hath taken the infection of the device, man.

MARIA. Nay, pursue him now, lest the device take air and taint.

FABIAN. Why, we shall make him mad indeed.

MARIA. The house will be the quieter.

SIR TOBY. Come, we 'll have him in a dark room and bound. My niece is already in the belief that he's mad: we may carry it thus, for our pleasure and his penance, till our very pastime, tired out of breath, prompt us to have mercy on him: at which time we will bring the device to the bar and crown thee for a finder of madmen. But see, but see.

Enter SIR ANDREW.]

FABIAN. More matter for a May morning.

110 **move**: make angry.

112 **used**: dealt with, handled.

113 **bawcock** (法语 beau coq): pretty cock, fine fellow.

114 **chuck**: chick.

116 **Biddy**: chickabiddy(逗鸡或逗婴儿语)。

117 **gravity**: a mature man. **cherry-pit**: children's game in which cherry stones are thrown into a small hole.

124 **element**: sphere, station, 身份, 地位。

129—130 **genius**: soul. **taken the infection of**: been affected by.

131—132 **device**: scheme. **take air and taint**: be exposed and spoilt.

137 **carry it**: play the game.

138 **tired out of breath**: exhausted of fun.

139—140 **bring / ... to the bar**: make public.

142 **matter for a May morning**: sport fit for a holiday.

SIR ANDREW. Here 's the challenge, read it: I warrant there 's vinegar and pepper in 't.

FABIAN. Is 't so saucy?

SIR ANDREW. Aye, is 't, I warrant him: do but read.

SIR TOBY. Give me. [*Reads*] Youth, whatsoever thou art, thou art but a scurvy fellow.

FABIAN. Good, and valiant.

SIR TOBY. [*Reads*] Wonder not, nor admire not in thy mind, why I do call thee so, for I will show thee no reason for 't.

FABIAN. A good note; that keeps you from the blow of the law.

SIR TOBY. [*Reads*] Thou comest to the lady Olivia, and in my sight she uses thee kindly: but thou liest in thy throat; that is not the matter I challenge thee for.

FABIAN. Very brief, and to exceeding good sense — less.

SIR TOBY. [*Reads*] I will waylay thee going home; where if it be thy chance to kill me, —

FABIAN. Good.

SIR TOBY. [*Reads*] Thou killest me like a rogue and a villain.

FABIAN. Still you keep o' the windy side of the law: good.

SIR TOBY. [*Reads*] Fare thee well; and God have mercy upon one of our souls! He may have mercy upon mine; but my hope is better, and so look to thyself. Thy friend, as thou usest him, and thy sworn enemy, ANDREW AGUECHEEK. If this letter move him not, his legs cannot; I'll give 't him.

MARIA. You may have very fit occasion for 't: he is now in some commerce with my lady, and will by and by depart.

SIR TOBY. Go, Sir Andrew; scout me for him at the corner of the orchard like a bum-baily: so soon as ever thou

145 **saucy**：①piquant；②important.

146 **him**：it.

150 **admire**：wonder.

153 **note**：observation，remark.

159 "less" is meant to be a suffix attached to the word "sense", by means of which all that is said previously is negated.

165 **o ' the windy side**：on the safe side.

169 **as thou usest him**：as your usage of him deserves (not at all).

170—171 **his / legs cannot**：his legs cannot move him.

173 **commerce**：conversation.

175 **scout me for him**：watch out for him (me 是语助词)。

176 **bum-baily**：sheriff's officer.

seest him, draw; and, as thou drawest, swear horrible; for it comes to pass oft that a terrible oath, with a swaggering accent sharply twanged off, gives manhood more approbation than ever proof itself would have earned him. Away!

SIR ANDREW. Nay, let me alone for swearing. [*Exit*.

SIR TOBY. Now will not I deliver his letter: for the behavior of the young gentleman gives him out to be of good capacity and breeding; his employment between his lord and my niece confirms no less: therefore this letter, being so excellently ignorant, will breed no terror in the youth: he will find it comes from a clodpole. But, sir, I will deliver his challenge by word of mouth; set upon Aguecheek a notable report of valor; and drive the gentleman, as I know his youth will aptly receive it, into a most hideous opinion of his rage, skill, fury and impetuosity. This will so fright them both, that they will kill one another by the look, like cockatrices.

Re-enter OLIVIA, *with* VIOLA.]

FABIAN. Here he comes with your niece: give them way till he take leave, and presently after him.

SIR TOBY. I will meditate the while upon some horrid message for a challenge. [*Exeunt* SIR TOBY, FABIAN, *and* MARIA.

OLIVIA. I have said too much unto a heart of stone,
And laid mine honor too unchary out:
There's something in me that reproves my fault;
But such a headstrong potent fault it is,
That it but mocks reproof.

VIOLA. With the same 'havior that your passion bears
Goes on my master's grief.

OLIVIA. Here, wear this jewel for me, 'tis my picture;
Refuse it not; it hath no tongue to vex you;

177 **draw**:拔剑。 **horrible**:horribly.

180 **approbation**:credit. **proof**:trial,testing.

182 **let me along for**:trust me for.

184 **gives him out**:shows him.

185 **capacity**:ability. **employment**:business.

189 **clodpole**:blockhead.

190 **set upon**:bestow on.

194 **by the look**:at the sight of each other.

195 **cockatrices**:传说中鸡身蛇尾的妖怪,它的目光可置人于死地。

196 **give them way**:get out of their way.

197 **presently after him**:then immediately go after him.

198 **horrid**:horrible.

201 **laid . . . out**:expended. **unchary**:carelessly.(out 在 1623 年对开本中作 on't,意思是 on the heart of stone,按伊丽莎白时代有在还债时把钱放在教堂里一块石头上的习惯做法。)

205 **With the same 'havior**:in the same manner. **bears**:carries on.

207 **jewel**:jewel-set miniature.

And I beseech you come again to-morrow.
What shall you ask of me that I'll deny,
That honor saved may upon asking give?

VIOLA. Nothing but this; — your true love for my master.

OLIVIA. How with mine honor may I give him that Which I have given to you ?

VIOLA. I will acquit you.

OLIVIA. Well, come again to-morrow: fare thee well: A fiend like thee might bear my soul to hell. [*Exit*.

Re-enter SIR TOBY *and* FABIAN.]

SIR TOBY. Gentleman, God save thee.

VIOLA. And you, sir.

SIR TOBY. That defense thou hast, betake thee to 't: of what nature the wrongs are thou hast done him, I know not; but thy interceptor, full of despite, bloody as the hunter, attends thee at the orchard-end: dismount thy tuck, be yare in thy preparation, for thy assailant is quick, skillful and deadly.

VIOLA. You mistake, sir; I am sure no man hath any quarrel to me: my remembrance is very free and clear from any image of offense done to any man.

SIR TOBY. You'll find it otherwise, I assure you: therefore, if you hold your life at any price, betake you to your guard; for your opposite hath in him what youth, strength, skill and wrath can furnish man withal.

VIOLA. I pray you, sir, what is he?

SIR TOBY. He is knight, dubbed with unhatched rapier and on carpet consideration; but he is a devil in private brawl: souls and bodies hath he divorced three; and his incensement at this moment is so implacable, that satisfaction can be none but by pangs of deaths and sepulcher. Hob, nob, is his word; give 't or take 't.

VIOLA. I will return again into the house and desire some

211 that honor may give, when asked for, without compromising itself.

221 **That defense thou hast**: such defense as you have. **betake thee to 't**: resort to it.

223 **despite**: spite.

224—225 **hunter**: hound. **attends**: waits for. **dismount thy tuck**: draw your sword. **yare**: ready, prompt.

228 **to**: with. **remembrance**: recollection.

232 **opposite**: opponent.

233 **withal**: with.

235 **dubbed**:被国王以剑按肩封为骑士或爵士的。 **unhatched**: not blunted.

236 **on carpet consideration**: for non-military service to the king (多半是献钱购得的爵位)。

237 **souls and bodies hath he divorced three**: he has deprived three bodies of their souls.

238 **incensement**: anger.

240 **Hob, nob**: have it or have it not, come what may.

conduct of the lady. I am no fighter. I have heard of some kind of men that put quarrels purposely on others, to taste their valor: belike this is a man of that quirk.

SIR TOBY. Sir, no; his indignation derives itself out of a very competent injury: therefore, get you on and give him his desire. Back you shall not to the house, unless you undertake that with me which with as much safety you might answer him: therefore, on, or strip your sword stark naked; for meddle you must, that's certain, or forswear to wear iron about you.

VIOLA. This is as uncivil as strange. I beseech you, do me this courteous office, as to know of the knight what my offense to him is: it is something of my negligence, nothing of my purpose.

SIR TOBY. I will do so. Signior Fabian, stay you by this gentleman till my return. [*Exit*.

VIOLA. Pray you, sir, do you know of this matter?

FABIAN. I know the knight is incensed against you, even to a mortal arbitrement; but nothing of the circumstance more.

VIOLA. I beseech you, what manner of man is he?

FABIAN. Nothing of that wonderful promise, to read him by his form, as you are like to find him in the proof of his valor. He is, indeed, sir, the most skillful, bloody and fatal opposite that you could possibly have found in any part of Illyria. Will you walk towards him? I will make your peace with him if I can.

VIOLA. I shall be much bound to you for 't: I am one that had rather go with sir priest than sir knight: I care not who knows so much of my mettle. [*Exeunt*.

Re-enter SIR TOBY, *with* SIR ANDREW.]

SIR TOBY. Why, man, he 's a very devil; I have not seen such a firago. I had a pass with him, rapier, scabbard and all, and he gives me the stuck in with such a mor-

242 conduct of: safe-conduct from.

244 taste: test. **belike**: perhaps. **quirk**: peculiar character.

246 competent: sufficient, adequate.

247—248 desire: satisfaction. **undertake that with me**: engage in fighting with me.

249—250 on: come on. **or strip your sword stark naked**: otherwise, disarm yourself. **meddle**: engage in combat.

251 wear iron about you: wear a sword.

253 know of: learn from.

254 it is: it must be.

255 purpose: intention.

260—261 mortal arbitrement: decision by a life-or-death combat. **nothing of the circumstance more**: nothing more about the circumstance.

263 Nothing of that wonderful promise: he doesn't look as terrible as he has been described to you. **read**: judge.

264 form: appearance.

266 opposite: opponent.

269 bound: obliged.

270 sir priest: 'sir' here stands for 'Dominus', the title given to a clergyman.

271 mettle: courage.

272 Why: 语气词。

273 firago: virago,剽悍的人(当时包括男女,后来专指女人)。

274 stuck in: thrust (from Italian 'stoccata').

tal motion, that it is inevitable; and on the answer, he pays you as surely as your feet hit the ground they step on. They say he has been fencer to the Sophy.

SIR ANDREW. Pox on 't, I'll not meddle with him.

SIR TOBY. Aye, but he will not now be pacified: Fabian can scarce hold him yonder.

SIR ANDREW. Plague on 't, an I thought he had been valiant and so cunning in fence I'ld have seen him damned ere I'ld have challenged him. Let him let the matter slip, and I 'll give him my horse, gray Capilet.

SIR TOBY. I'll make the motion: stand here, make a good show on 't: this shall end without the perdition of souls. [*Aside*] Marry, I'll ride your horse as well as I ride you. *Re-enter* FABIAN *and* VIOLA.]

[*To* FABIAN.] I have his horse to take up the quarrel: I have persuaded him the youth 's a devil.

FABIAN. He is as horribly conceited of him; and pants and looks pale, as if a bear were at his heels.

SIR TOBY. [*To* VIOLA.] There 's no remedy, sir; he will fight with you for 's oath sake: marry, he hath better bethought him of his quarrel, and he finds that now scarce to be worth talking of: therefore draw, for the supportance of his vow; he protests he will not hurt you.

VIOLA. [*Aside*] Pray God defend me! A little thing would make me tell them how much I lack of a man.

FABIAN. Give ground, if you see him furious.

SIR TOBY. Come, Sir Andrew, there's no remedy; the gentleman will, for his honor's sake, have one bout with you; he cannot by the duello avoid it : but he has promised me, as he is a gentleman and a soldier, he will not hurt you. Come on; to 't.

SIR ANDREW. Pray God, he keep his oath!

VIOLA. I do assure you, 'tis against my will. [*They draw. Enter* ANTONIO.]

275—276 **inevitable**: impossible to evade. **on the answer, he pays you**: he counters your return blow.

277 **Sophy**: 波斯国王，见 II. v 173 行。

278 **Pox**: plague, curse. **meddle**: engage in combat.

281 **an**: if.

282 **I'ld**: I would.

283 **I'ld**: I should.

284 **slip**: be forgotten.

285 **make the motion**: put forward the proposal.

286 **perdition**: loss.

287—288 **Marry**: by Mary(诅咒语)。(第二个)**ride**: rule over.

289 **take up**: make up.

291 **is as horribly conceited**: has as terrifying an idea.

294—295 **for 's oath sake**: (oath 后省略 's) for the sake of the oath he has made. **he hath better bethought him of his quarrel**: he has reconsidered and is seeing the quarrel in a more reasonable light.

295 **that**: the quarrel.

296—297 **supportance**: maintenance.

302 **bout**: round or turn in fencing.

303 **duello**: established code of duelling.

ANTONIO. Put up your sword. If this young gentleman
Have done offense, I take the fault on me:
If you offend him, I for him defy you.

SIR TOBY. You, sir! why, what are you?

ANTONIO. One, sir, that for his love dares yet do more
Than you have heard him brag to you he will.

SIR TOBY. Nay, if you be an undertaker, I am for you.
[*They draw*.

Enter OFFICERS.]

FABIAN. O good Sir Toby, hold! here come the officers.

SIR TOBY. I 'll be with you anon.

VIOLA. Pray, sir, put your sword up, if you please.

SIR ANDREW. Marry, will I, sir; and, for that I promised you, I'll be as good as my word: he will bear you easily and reins well.

FIRST OFFICER. This is the man; do thy office.

SECOND OFFICER. Antonio, I arrest thee at the suit of Count Orsino.

ANTONIO. You do mistake me, sir.

FIRST OFFICER. No, sir, no jot; I know your favor well, Though now you have no sea-cap on your head. Take him away: he knows I know him well.

ANTONIO. I must obey. [*To* VIOLA.] This comes with seeking you:
But there 's no remedy; I shall answer it.
What will you do, now my necessity
Makes me to ask you for my purse? It grieves me
Much more for what I cannot do for you
Than what befalls myself. You stand amazed;
But be of comfort.

SECOND OFFICER. Come, sir, away.

ANTONIO. I must entreat of you some of that money.

VIOLA. What money, sir?
For the fair kindness you have show'd me here, And,

314 **undertaker**: meddler.

316 **anon**: at once.

318 that I promised (the horse).

319 **be as good as my word**: keep my promise. **he**: it.

325 **favor**: face.

335 **be of comfort**: rest at ease.

337 **entreat of you**: ask from you.

part, being prompted by your present trouble,
Out of my lean and low ability
I'll lend you something: my having is not much;
I'll make division of my present with you:
Hold, there 's half my coffer.

ANTONIO. Will you deny me now?
Is 't possible that my deserts to you
Can lack persuasion? Do not tempt my misery,
Lest that it make me so unsound a man
As to upbraid you with those kindnesses
That I have done for you.

VIOLA. I know of none;
Nor know I you by voice or any feature:
I hate ingratitude more in a man
Than lying vainness, babbling drunkenness,
Or any taint of vice whose strong corruption
Inhabits our frail blood.

ANTONIO. O heavens themselves!

SECOND OFFICER. Come, sir, I pray you, go.

ANTONIO. Let me speak a little. This youth that you see
here I snatch'd one half out of the jaws of death;
Relieved him with such sanctity of love;
And to his image, which methought did promise
Most venerable worth, did I devotion.

FIRST OFFICER. What's that to us? The time goes by: away!

ANTONIO. But O how vile an idol proves this god!
Thou hast, Sebastian, done good feature shame.
In nature there 's no blemish but the mind;
None can be call'd deform'd but the unkind:
Virtue is beauty; but the beauteous evil
Are empty trunks, o'erflourish'd by the devil.

FIRST OFFICER. The man grows mad: away with him!
Come, come, sir.

ANTONIO. Lead me on. [*Exit with* OFFICERS.

340 **part**: partly. **prompted**: moved.

341 **lean and low**: scanty. **ability**: wealth, means.

342 **having**: resources.

343 **my present**: my present store.

344 **coffer**: chest 转义 purse.

345 **deny**: disown.

346 **deserts to you**: rightful claims to your kindness.

347 **persuasion**: persuasiveness. **tempt**: make trial of.

354 **vainness**: boasting.

360 **one half**: nearly.

361 **sanctity of love**: pure love.

362—363 I gave loyalty to his image, which I thought promised most honorable worth.

370 **trunks, o'erflourish'd**:伊丽莎白时代的箱子上常画着或刻着花朵。

VIOLA. Methinks his words do from such passion fly,
That he believes himself: so do not I.
Prove true, imagination, O prove true,
That I, dear brother, be now ta'en for you!

SIR TOBY. Come hither, knight; come hither, Fabian: we 'll whisper o'er a couplet or two of most sage saws.

VIOLA. He named Sebastian: I my brother know
Yet living in my glass; even such and so
In favor was my brother, and he went
Still in this fashion, color, ornament,
For him I imitate: O, if it prove,
Tempests are kind and salt waves fresh in love! [*Exit*.

SIR TOBY. A very dishonest paltry boy, and more a coward than a hare: his dishonesty appears in leaving his friend here in necessity and denying him; and for his cowardship, ask Fabian.

FABIAN. A coward, a most devout coward, religious in it.

SIR ANDREW. 'Slid, I 'll after him again and beat him.

SIR TOBY. Do; cuff him soundly, but never draw thy sword.

SIR ANDREW. An I do not, — [*Exit*.

FABIAN. Come, let's see the event.

SIR TOBY. I dare lay any money 'twill be nothing yet.

[*Exeunt*.

375 **so do not I**: but I do not believe him.

377 **ta'en**: mistaken.

379 **o'er**: through the duration of. 即让 Viola 去讲两句双行押韵的格言吧。**sage saws**: wise adages.

381 **glass**: image.

382 **favor**: face.

383 **Still**: always.

386 **dishonest**: dishonorable. **paltry**: worthless.

390 **devout**: persistent. **religious**: strict, scrupulous, conscientious.

392 **'Slid**: by God's eyelid(一种咒骂语)。

394 **An**: if.

395 **event**: result.

396 **lay**: wager. **yet**: after all.

ACT IV

SCENE I

—Before OLIVIA'S *house.*

Enter SEBASTIAN *and* CLOWN.]

CLOWN. Will you make me believe that I am not sent for you?

SEBASTIAN. Go to, go to, thou art a foolish fellow: Let me be clear of thee.

CLOWN. Well held out, i' faith! No, I do not know you; nor I am not sent to you by my lady, to bid you come speak with her; nor your name is not Master Cesario; nor this is not my nose neither. Nothing that is so is so.

SEBASTIAN. I prithee, vent thy folly somewhere else:
Thou know'st not me.

CLOWN. Vent my folly! he has heard that word of some great man and now applies it to a fool. Vent my folly! I am afraid this great lubber, the world, will prove a cockney. I prithee now, ungird thy strangeness and tell me what I shall vent to my lady: shall I vent to her that thou art coming?

SEBASTIAN. I prithee, foolish Greek, depart from me:
There's money for thee: if you tarry longer,
I shall give worse payment.

CLOWN. By my troth, thou hast an open hand. These wise men that give fools money get themselves a good report — after fourteen years' purchase.

Enter SIR ANDREW, SIR TOBY, *and* FABIAN.]

SIR ANDREW. Now, sir, have I met you again? there's

IV. i

4 clear of：rid of.

5 held out：kept up.

6—7 nor I am not：这种双重否定式，在当时并不少见。**come speak**：come and speak，(or) come to speak.

10 vent：①void，get rid of；②utter，give expression to.

12 of：from.

14 lubber：overgrown boy.

15 cockney：effeminate or foppish fellow. **ungird**：relax. **strangeness**：stand-offishness.

18 foolish Greek：merry Greek，buffoon.

23 after fourteen years' purchase：at a price (at a price equivalent to fourteen years' annual rent，当时一般地价合 12 年租金)。

24—25 there's for you：there's a blow for you.

for you.

SEBASTIAN. Why, there 's for thee, and there, and there. Are all the people mad?

SIR TOBY. Hold, sir, or I'll throw your dagger o'er the house.

CLOWN. This will I tell my lady straight: I would not be in some of your coats for two pence. [*Exit.*

SIR TOBY. Come on, sir; hold.

SIR ANDREW. Nay, let him alone: I'll go another way to work with him; I'll have an action of battery against him, if there be any law in Illyria: though I struck him first, yet it 's no matter for that.

SEBASTIAN. Let go thy hand.

SIR TOBY. Come, sir, I will not let you go. Come, my young soldier, put up your iron: you are well fleshed; come on.

SEBASTIAN. I will be free from thee. What wouldst thou now? If thou darest tempt me further, draw thy sword.

SIR TOBY. What, what? Nay, then I must have an ounce or two of this malapert blood from you.

Enter OLIVIA.]

OLIVIA. Hold, Toby; on thy life, I charge thee, hold!

SIR TOBY. Madam!

OLIVIA. Will it be ever thus? Ungracious wretch,
Fit for the mountains and the barbarous caves,
Where manners ne'er were preach'd! out of my sight!
Be not offended, dear Cesario.
Rudesby, be gone!

[*Exeunt* SIR TOBY, SIR ANDREW, *and* FABIAN.

I prithee, gentle friend,
Let thy fair wisdom, not thy passion, sway
In this uncivil and unjust extent
Against thy peace. Go with me to my house;
And hear thou there how many fruitless pranks

30 — 31 **straight**: directly. **be in ... your coats**: stand in your shoes.

34 **work with**: cope with. **action**: legal process. **battery**: assault.

39 **iron**: sword. **fleshed**: initiated into fighting.

44 **malapert**: impudent, saucy.

45 **on thy life, I charge thee**: either you obey my order, or you forfeit your life.

51 **Rudesby**: unmannerly fellow.

54 **extent**: attack, assault.

This ruffian hath botch'd up, that thou thereby
Mayst smile at this: thou shalt not choose but go:
Do not deny. Beshrew his soul for me,
He started one poor heart of mine in thee.

SEBASTIAN. What relish is in this? how runs the stream?
Or I am mad, or else this is a dream:
Let fancy still my sense in Lethe steep;
If it be thus to dream, still let me sleep!

OLIVIA. Nay, come, I prithee: would thou 'ldst be ruled by me!

SEBASTIAN. Madam, I will.

OLIVIA. O, say so, and so be! [*Exeunt*.

SCENE II

—OLIVIA'S *house*.

Enter MARIA *and* CLOWN.]

MARIA. Nay, I prithee, put on this gown and this beard; make him believe thou art Sir Topas the curate: do it quickly; I'll call Sir Toby the whilst. [*Exit*.

CLOWN. Well, I'll put it on, and I will dissemble myself in 't; and I would I were the first that ever dissembled in such a gown. I am not tall enough to become the function well, nor lean enough to be thought a good student; but to be said an honest man and a good housekeeper goes as fairly as to say a careful man and a great scholar. The competitors enter.

Enter SIR TOBY *and* MARIA.]

SIR TOBY. Jove bless thee, master Parson.

CLOWN. Bonos dies, Sir Toby; for, as the old hermit of Prague, that never saw pen and ink, very wittily said to a niece of King Gorboduc, 'That that is is;' so I, being master Parson, am master Parson; for, what is 'that' but 'that,' and 'is' but 'is'?

57 **botch'd up**:clumsily contrived.

59 **deny**:refuse. **Beshrew**:curse.

60 **started**:roused(打猎用语)。 **heart**:①心;②鹿。 **in thee**:诗喻,情人互换心脏,故"你胸中有我心"。

61 **relish**:taste. **What relish is in this?**:What am I to make of this? **how runs the stream?**:how goes the trend?

62 **Or**:either.

63 Let love steep my sense always in Lethe(希腊神话地狱中一条河,饮其水即忘记过去)。

65 **would**:I wish.

IV. ii

2 **Sir**:神职人员的尊称。 **Topas**:topaz,黄玉(传说能治疯病)。**curate**:教区牧师助理。

3 **the whilst**:in the meantime.

5 **would**:wish. 此句有讽刺教士之义,指教士作假,久已有之。

6 **become**:suit.

7 **function**:office.

8 **said**:called.

9 **goes as fairly as to say**:is just as well as being called.

10 **competitors**:confederates,partners.

12 **Bonos dies**(假冒拉丁语):good day.

13 **Prague**:布拉格(地名)。

14 **Gorboduc**:传说中古英国国王,有名的 16 世纪剧本的主角。文中的这些话都是随意编的。

SIR TOBY. To him, Sir Topas.

CLOWN. What, ho, I say! peace in this prison!

SIR TOBY. The knave counterfeits well; a good knave.

MALVOLIO. [*Within*] Who calls there?

CLOWN. Sir Topas the curate, who comes to visit Malvolio the lunatic.

MALVOLIO. Sir Topas, Sir Topas, good Sir Topas, go to my lady.

CLOWN. Out, hyperbolical fiend! how vexest thou this man! talkest thou nothing but of ladies?

SIR TOBY. Well said, master Parson.

MALVOLIO. Sir Topas, never was man thus wronged: good Sir Topas, do not think I am mad: they have laid me here in hideous darkness.

CLOWN. Fie, thou dishonest Satan! I call thee by the most modest terms; for I am one of those gentle ones that will use the devil himself with courtesy: sayest thou that house is dark?

MALVOLIO. As hell, Sir Topas.

CLOWN. Why, it hath bay windows transparent as barricadoes, and the clearstories toward the south north are as lustrous as ebony; and yet complainest thou of obstruction?

MALVOLIO. I am not mad, Sir Topas: I say to you, this house is dark.

CLOWN. Madman, thou errest: I say, there is no darkness but ignorance; in which thou art more puzzled than the Egyptians in their fog.

MALVOLIO. I say, this house is as dark as ignorance, though ignorance were as dark as hell; and I say, there was never man thus abused. I am no more mad than you are: make the trial of it in any constant question.

CLOWN. What is the opinion of Pythagoras concerning wild fowl?

20 MALVOLIO. [*Within*]：他在台后部的囚室中。

25 hyperbolical：boisterous.

33 use：treat.

36—37 bay windows：墙上凸出的大窗，三面有玻璃，是当时正流行的建筑设施。 **barricadoes**：路障（其实并不透光，是反话）。

37 clearstories：天窗。

38—39 obstruction：shutting out of light.

44 Egyptians in their fog：埃及三天黑暗之灾，见《圣经·旧约·出埃及记》第 10 章 21 节起。

48 constant question：formally conducted discussion.

49 Pythagoras：毕达哥拉斯是公元前六世纪的希腊哲学家。他主张“灵魂轮回”，并认为畜牲的灵魂可投胎进入人的躯体。

MALVOLIO. That the soul of our grandam might haply inhabit a bird.

CLOWN. What thinkest thou of his opinion?

MALVOLIO. I think nobly of the soul, and no way approve his opinion.

CLOWN. Fare thee well. Remain thou still in darkness: thou shalt hold the opinion of Pythagoras ere I will allow of thy wits; and fear to kill a woodcock, lest thou dispossess the soul of thy grandam. Fare thee well.

MALVOLIO. Sir Topas, Sir Topas!

SIR TOBY. My most exquisite Sir Topas!

CLOWN. Nay, I am for all waters.

MARIA. Thou mightst have done this without thy beard and gown: he sees thee not.

SIR TOBY. To him in thine own voice, and bring me word how thou findest him: I would we were well rid of this knavery. If he may be conveniently delivered, I would he were; for I am now so far in offense with my niece, that I cannot pursue with any safety this sport to the upshot. Come by and by to my chamber.

[*Exeunt* SIR TOBY *and* MARIA.

CLOWN. [*Singing*] Hey, Robin, jolly Robin,
Tell me how thy lady does.

MALVOLIO. Fool, —

CLOWN. My lady is unkind, perdy.

MALVOLIO. Fool, —

CLOWN. Alas, why is she so?

MALVOLIO. Fool, I say, —

CLOWN. She loves another — Who calls, ha?

MALVOLIO. Good fool, as ever thou wilt deserve well at my hand, help me to a candle, and pen, ink and paper: as I am a gentleman, I will live to be thankful to thee for 't.

CLOWN. Master Malvolio!

51 **grandam**：grand mother. **haply**：perhaps.

54 **no way**：in no way.

57 **ere**：before.

58 **allow of**：grant，admit.

59 **dispossess**：dislodge.

62 **for all waters**：ready for anything. **waters**：宝石的光泽度。

65 **To him in thine own voice**：go to him and speak to him in your own voice.

66 **would**（下一行的 would 同）：wish.

67 **knavery**：roguish trick（i. e.，making sport of Malvolio）.

70 **upshot**：decisive shot（箭术用语），conclusion.

71 歌五（1）、（2），见 174—176 页。

74 **perdy**：（an oath）by God.

MALVOLIO. Aye, good fool.

CLOWN. Alas, sir, how fell you besides your five wits?

MALVOLIO. Fool, there was never man so notoriously abused: I am as well in my wits, fool, as thou art.

CLOWN. But as well? then you are mad indeed, if you be no better in your wits than a fool.

MALVOLIO. They have here propertied me; keep me in darkness, send ministers to me, asses, and do all they can to face me out of my wits.

CLOWN. Advise you what you say; the minister is here. Malvolio, Malvolio, thy wits the heavens restore! endeavor thyself to sleep, and leave thy vain bibble babble.

MALVOLIO. Sir Topas, —

CLOWN. Maintain no words with him, good fellow. Who, I, sir? not I, sir. God be wi' you, good Sir Topas. Marry, amen. I will, sir, I will.

MALVOLIO. Fool, fool, fool, I say, —

CLOWN. Alas, sir, be patient. What say you, sir? I am shent for speaking to you.

MALVOLIO. Good fool, help me to some light and some paper: I tell thee, I am as well in my wits as any man in Illyria.

CLOWN. Well-a-day that you were, sir!

MALVOLIO. By this hand, I am. Good fool, some ink, paper and light ; and convey what I will set down to my lady: it shall advantage thee more than ever the bearing of letter did.

CLOWN. I will help you to 't. But tell me true, are you not mad indeed? or do you but counterfeit?

MALVOLIO. Believe me, I am not; I tell thee true.

CLOWN. Nay, I'll ne'er believe a madman till I see his brains. I will fetch you light and paper and ink.

MALVOLIO. Fool, I'll requite it in the highest degree: I

85 fell ... besides your five wits: became out of your mind (five wits: common sense, imagination, fancy, estimation, memory).

88 But as well?: only like me?

90 propertied: treated as a mere property.

92 face: bully, brazen.

93 Advise you: be careful.

94 may the heavens restore your wits!

95—96 endeavor thyself to sleep: try to go to sleep. **leave**: stop. **bibble babble**: prattle.

98—100 Maintain no words: do not make conversation. **CLOWN**: 先学牧师助理口气,后用自己口音讲话。

103 shent: blamed, rebuked.

107 Well-a-day: alas. **that you were**: I wish that you were.

110 advantage (v.): profit.

117 requite: repay.

prithee, be gone.

CLOWN. [*Singing*] I am gone, sir.
And anon, sir,
I'll be with you again,
In a trice,
Like to the old vice,
Your need to sustain;
Who, with dagger of lath,
In his rage and his wrath,
Cries, ah, ha! to the devil:
Like a mad lad,
Pare thy nails, dad;
Adieu, goodman devil. [*Exit*.

SCENE III

—OLIVIA'S *garden*.

Enter SEBASTIAN.]

SEBASTIAN. This is the air; that is the glorious sun;
This pearl she gave me, I do feel 't and see 't;
And though 'tis wonder that enwraps me thus,
Yet 'tis not madness. Where 's Antonio, then?
I could not find him at the Elephant:
Yet there he was; and there I found this credit,
That he did range the town to seek me out.
His counsel now might do me golden service;
For though my soul disputes well with my sense,
That this may be some error, but not madness,
Yet doth this accident and flood of fortune
So far exceed all instance, all discourse,
That I am ready to distrust mine eyes
And wrangle with my reason, that persuades me
To any other trust but that I am mad,
Or else the lady's mad; yet, if 'twere so,

122 **trice**：moment of time.

123 **Like to**：like. **old vice**：中世纪道德剧中“罪恶”这一角色，后来有些丑角是从此演变而来。

124 **sustain**：support.

125 **Who**：指 old vice. **dagger of lath**：木制匕首，用以假装削指甲，是道德剧一段戏。

IV. iii

6 **there he was**：he had been there. **credit**：report.

7 **range**：traverse.

8 **golden**：precious.

12 **instance**：past example. **discourse**：reasoning.

14 **persuades**：urges.

15 **trust**：belief，conviction.

She could not sway her house, command her followers,
Take and give back affairs and their dispatch
With such a smooth, discreet, and stable bearing
As I perceive she does: there's something in 't
That is deceivable. But here the lady comes.

Enter OLIVIA *and* PRIEST.]

OLIVIA. Blame not this haste of mine. If you mean well,
Now go with me and with this holy man
Into the chantry by: there, before him,
And underneath that consecrated roof,
Plight me the full assurance of your faith;
That my most jealous and too doubtful soul
May live at peace. He shall conceal it
Whiles you are willing it shall come to note,
What time we will our celebration keep
According to my birth. What do you say?

SEBASTIAN. I'll follow this good man, and go with you;
And having sworn truth, ever will be true.

OLIVIA. Then lead the way, good father; and heavens so shine,
That they may fairly note this act of mine! [*Exeunt*.

17 **sway**: rule.

18 **Take and give back**: handle. **their dispatch**: the settlement of the affairs.

21 **deceivable**: deceptive, deceitful.

24 **chantry**: chapel. **by**: nearby.

26 **Plight**: pledge.

27 **That**: so that.

29 **Whiles**: till. **come to note**: come to be known.

31 **birth**: rank.

36 **note**: notice, witness.

ACT V

SCENE I

—*Before* OLIVIA'S *house*.

Enter CLOWN *and* FABIAN.]

FABIAN. Now, as thou lovest me, let me see his letter.

CLOWN. Good Master Fabian, grant me another request.

FABIAN. Any thing.

CLOWN. Do not desire to see this letter.

FABIAN. This is, to give a dog, and in recompense desire my dog again.

Enter DUKE, VIOLA, CURIO, *and* LORDS.]

DUKE. Belong you to the Lady Olivia, friends?

CLOWN. Aye, sir; we are some of her trappings.

DUKE. I know thee well: how dost thou, my good fellow?

CLOWN. Truly, sir, the better for my foes and the worse for my friends.

DUKE. Just the contrary; the better for thy friends.

CLOWN. No, sir, the worse.

DUKE. How can that be?

CLOWN. Marry, sir, they praise me and make an ass of me; now my foes tell me plainly I am an ass: so that by my foes, sir, I profit in the knowledge of myself; and by my friends I am abused: so that, conclusions to be as kisses, if your four negatives make your two affirmatives, why then, the worse for my friends, and the better for my foes.

DUKE. Why, this is excellent.

CLOWN. By my troth, sir, no; though it please you to be

V. i

5—6 这是实有此事。据说英女王向 Dr. Bulleyn 索要他心爱的狗，允许满足他的一个要求作为回报，Dr. Bulleyn 即以索还狗作为他的要求。

9 **trappings**：ornaments 转义 followers.

11 **for**：because of，on account of.

19—21 **abused**：deceived. **conclusions ... affirmatives**：conclusions based on the assumptions that，when asked to be kissed，a girl's "No，no，no，no！"could be interpreted as "Yes，yes！".

one of my friends.

DUKE. Thou shalt not be the worse for me: there's gold.

CLOWN. But that it would be double-dealing, sir, I would you could make it another.

DUKE. O, you give me ill counsel.

CLOWN. Put your grace in your pocket, sir, for this once, and let your flesh and blood obey it.

DUKE. Well, I will be so much a sinner, to be a double-dealer: there 's another.

CLOWN. Primo, secundo, tertio, is a good play; and the old saying is, the third pays for all: the triplex, sir, is a good tripping measure; or the bells of Saint Bennet, sir, may put you in mind; one, two, three.

DUKE. You can fool no more money out of me at this throw: if you will let your lady know I am here to speak with her, and bring her along with you, it may awake my bounty further.

CLOWN. Marry, sir, lullaby to your bounty till I come again. I go, sir; but I would not have you to think that my desire of having is the sin of covetousness: but, as you say, sir, let your bounty take a nap, I will awake it anon. [*Exit*.

VIOLA. Here comes the man, sir, that did rescue me.

Enter ANTONIO *and* OFFICERS.]

DUKE. That face of his I do remember well;
Yet, when I saw it last, it was besmear'd
As black as Vulcan in the smoke of war:
A bawbling vessel was he captain of,
For shallow draught and bulk unprizable;
With which such scathful grapple did he make
With the most noble bottom of our fleet,
That very envy and the tongue of loss
Cried fame and honor on him. What's the matter?

FIRST OFFICER. Orsino, this is that Antonio

27 But that:except that. **double-dealing**:①两面派行为;②双倍赏钱。

30 your grace:①公爵大人;②你所得的神的恩惠。

33 there 's another:又给了一份赏钱。

34 Primo, secundo, tertio〈拉丁语〉:第一,第二,第三。

35 triplex:triple time (in music).

36 tripping measure:dancing step. **Saint Bennet**:伦敦 St. Benedict 教堂。

38—39 this throw:这一次(第三次)掷的骰子。

42 lullaby to:愿它安睡。

50 Vulcan:罗马神话中的铁匠神。

51 bawbling:trifling.

52 For:fit for. **draught**:吃水。 **bulk**:hull of a ship. **unprizable**:worthless.

53 scathful:harmful. **grapple**:struggle.

54 bottom:ship.

55 loss:losers.

That took the Phœnix and her fraught from Candy;
And this is he that did the Tiger board,
When your young nephew Titus lost his leg:
Here in the streets, desperate of shame and state,
In private brabble did we apprehend him.

VIOLA. He did me kindness, sir, drew on my side;
But in conclusion put strange speech upon me:
I know not what 't was but distraction.

DUKE. Notable pirate! thou salt-water thief!
What foolish boldness brought thee to their mercies,
Whom thou, in terms so bloody and so dear,
Hast made thine enemies?

ANTONIO. Orsino, noble sir,
Be pleased that I shake off these names you give me:
Antonio never yet was thief or pirate,
Though I confess, on base and ground enough,
Orsino's enemy. A witchcraft drew me hither:
That most ingrateful boy there by your side,
From the rude sea's enraged and foamy mouth
Did I redeem; a wreck past hope he was:
His life I gave him and did thereto add
My love, without retention or restraint,
All his in dedication; for his sake
Did I expose myself, pure for his love,
Into the danger of this adverse town;
Drew to defend him when he was beset:
Where being apprehended, his false cunning,
Not meaning to partake with me in danger,
Taught him to face me out of his acquaintance,
And grew a twenty years removèd thing
While one would wink; denied me mine own purse,
Which I had recommended to his use
Not half an hour before.

VIOLA. How can this be?

58 **Phœnix**: the name of a ship. **fraught**: freight, cargo. **Candy**: Candia (now Crete).

59 **Tiger**: the name of a ship.

61 **desperate**: reckless, utterly careless of. **shame and state**: harm to his name and position.

62 **brabble**: brawl. **apprehend**: arrest.

63 **drew**: fought with sword. **on my side**: in my defense.

64 **in conclusion**: finally. **put strange speech upon me**: spoke to me in a strange manner.

65 **distraction**: mental derangement.

67 **mercies**: power.

68 **in terms**: in the manner. **dear**: grievous, dire.

71 **shake off**: refuse to accept.

75 **ingrateful**: ungrateful.

76 **rude**: turbulent, rough.

77 **wreck**: shipwrecked person.

79 **without retention or restraint**: without reserve.

81 **pure**: purely.

82 **adverse**: hostile.

83 **beset**: attacked.

86 **face me out of**: deny to my face.

87 **removèd thing**: estranged being.

88 **While one would wink**: in a wink.

89 **recommended**: consigned, committed.

DUKE. When came he to this town?

ANTONIO. To-day, my lord; and for three months before,
No interim, not a minute's vacancy,
Both day and night did we keep company.

Enter OLIVIA *and* ATTENDANTS.]

DUKE. Here comes the countess: now heaven walks on earth.
But for thee, fellow; fellow, thy words are madness:
Three months this youth hath tended upon me;
But more of that anon. Take him aside.

OLIVIA. What would my lord, but that he may not have,
Wherein Olivia may seem serviceable?
Cesario, you do not keep promise with me.

VIOLA. Madam!

DUKE. Gracious Olivia, —

OLIVIA. What do you say, Cesario? Good my lord, —

VIOLA. My lord would speak; my duty hushes me.

OLIVIA. If it be aught to the old tune, my lord,
It is as fat and fulsome to mine ear
As howling after music.

DUKE. Still so cruel?

OLIVIA. Still so constant, lord.

DUKE. What, to perverseness? you uncivil lady,
To whose ingrate and unauspicious altars
My soul the faithful'st offerings hath breathed out
That e'er devotion tender'd! What shall I do?

OLIVIA. Even what it please my lord, that shall become him.

DUKE. Why should I not, had I the heart to do it,
Like to the Egyptian thief at point of death,
Kill what I love? — a savage jealousy
That sometimes savors nobly. But hear me this:
Since you to non-regardance cast my faith,
And that I partly know the instrument

93 **three months**:实际上,只有几天的时间。

99 **tended upon**: waited or attended upon.

106 **Good my lord**: a polite request to Orsino to let Viola speak first.

109 **fat and fulsome**: tiresome, nauseating.

114 **ingrate**: ungrateful.

117 **become**: befit.

118 **him**: my lord.

120 **Egyptian thief**: Theagenes 企图杀死他所爱的 Charicleia,以免她落入强人之手,事见 Heliodorus 的 *Aethiopica*,当时有英文译本。**at point of death**: about to die.

122 **savors nobly**: has a noble quality about it.

123 **non-regardance**: disregard.

124 **instrument**: agent.

That screws me from my true place in your favor,
Live you the marble-breasted tyrant still;
But this your minion, whom I know you love,
And whom, by heaven I swear, I tender dearly,
Him will I tear out of that cruel eye,
Where he sits crowned in his master's spite.
Come, boy, with me; my thoughts are ripe in mischief:
I'll sacrifice the lamb that I do love,
To spite a raven's heart within a dove.
VIOLA. And I, most jocund, apt and willingly,
To do you rest, a thousand deaths would die.
OLIVIA. Where goes Cesario?
VIOLA. After him I love
More than I love these eyes, more than my life,
More, by all mores, than e'er I shall love wife.
If I do feign, you witnesses above
Punish my life for tainting of my love!
OLIVIA. Aye me, detested! how am I beguiled!
VIOLA. Who does beguile you? who does do you wrong?
OLIVIA. Hast thou forgot thyself? is it so long?
Call forth the holy father.
DUKE. Come, away!
OLIVIA. Whither, my lord? Cesario, husband, stay.
DUKE. Husband!
OLIVIA. Aye, husband: can he that deny?
DUKE. Her husband, sirrah!
VIOLA. No, my lord, not I.
OLIVIA. Alas, it is the baseness of thy fear
That makes thee strangle thy propriety:
Fear not, Cesario; take thy fortunes up;
Be that thou know'st thou art, and then thou art
As great as that thou fear'st.
Enter PRIEST.]
O, welcome, father!

125 **screws**：wrenches.

126 **marble-breasted**：hard-hearted. **still**：always.

127 **minion**：darling，favorite.

128 **tender**：have a tender regard for，care for.

130 **in his master's spite**：to the mortification of his master.

133 **spite**：vex，mortify.

135 **do you rest**：give you repose.

139 **by all mores**：①by all standards；②by all "mores". beyond all comparisons.

140 **you witnesses above**：gods in heaven.

142 **Aye**：alas. **detested**：(I am) detested. **beguiled**：deceived.

150 **sirrah**：a contemptuous mode of address.

153 **strangle thy propriety**：suppress your identity as my husband，suppress the fact that I am yours.

Father, I charge thee, by thy reverence,
Here to unfold, though lately we intended
To keep in darkness what occasion now
Reveals before 'tis ripe, what thou dost know
Hath newly pass'd between this youth and me.

PRIEST. A contract of eternal bond of love,
Confirm'd by mutual joinder of your hands,
Attested by the holy close of lips,
Strengthen'd by interchangement of your rings;
And all the ceremony of this compact
Seal'd in my function, by my testimony:
Since when, my watch hath told me, toward my grave
I have travel'd but two hours.

DUKE. O thou dissembling cub! what wilt thou be
When time hath sow'd a grizzle on thy case?
Or will not else thy craft so quickly grow,
That thine own trip shall be thine overthrow?
Farewell, and take her; but direct thy feet
Where thou and I henceforth may never meet.

VIOLA. My lord, I do protest —

OLIVIA. O, do not swear!
Hold little faith, though thou hast too much fear.

Enter SIR ANDREW.]

SIR ANDREW. For the love of God, a surgeon! Send one presently to Sir Toby.

OLIVIA. What's the matter?

SIR ANDREW. He has broke my head across and has given Sir Toby a bloody coxcomb too: for the love of God, your help! I had rather than forty pound I were at home.

OLIVIA. Who has done this, Sir Andrew?

SIR ANDREW. The count's gentleman, one Cesario: we took him for a coward, but he's the very devil incardinate.

159 **unfold**：disclose.

160 **occasion**：necessity.

164 **joinder**：joining.

165 **close of lips**：kiss.

168 **function**：office.

171 **cub**：ill-mannered young man.

172 **grizzle**：sprinkling of grey hairs. **case**：skin.

174 **trip**：①misstep；②headlong speed.

179 **little**：a little.

181 **presently**：at once.

183 **broke**：broken.

184 **coxcomb**：head.

185—186 **I had rather than forty pound I were at / home**：I had rather be at home than have forty pounds.

189—190 **incardinate**：Sir Andrew's error for 'incarnate'.

DUKE. My gentleman,Cesario?

SIR ANDREW. 'Od's lifelings, here he is! You broke my head for nothing;and that that I did,I was set on to do 't by Sir Toby.

VIOLA. Why do you speak to me? I never hurt you:
You drew your sword upon me without cause;
But I bespake you fair,and hurt you not.

SIR ANDREW. If a bloody coxcomb be a hurt,you have hurt me:I think you set nothing by a bloody coxcomb.

Enter SIR TOBY *and* CLOWN.]

Here comes Sir Toby halting; you shall hear more: but if he had not been in drink, he would have tickled you other gates than he did.

DUKE. How now,gentleman! how is 't with you?

SIR TOBY. That's all one:has hurt me,and there's the end on 't. Sot,didst see Dick surgeon,sot?

CLOWN. O, he's drunk,Sir Toby, an hour agone; his eyes were set at eight i' the morning.

SIR TOBY. Then he's a rogue, and a passy measures pavin: I hate a drunken rogue.

OLIVIA. Away with him! Who hath made this havoc with them?

SIR ANDREW. I'll help you, Sir Toby, because we'll be dressed together.

SIR TOBY. Will you help? an ass-head and a coxcomb and a knave,a thin-faced knave,a gull!

OLIVIA. Get him to bed, and let his hurt be look'd to.

[*Exeunt* CLOWN,FABIAN,SIR TOBY *and* SIR ANDREW.

Enter SEBASTIAN.]

SEBASTIAN. I am sorry,madam,I have hurt your kinsman;
But,had it been the brother of my blood,
I must have done no less with wit and safety.
You throw a strange regard upon me,and by that
I do perceive it hath offended you:

192 'Od's lifelings: God's life, a trivial oath.

193—194 that that ... / 't: what.

197 bespake: spoke to. **fair**: civilly, courteously.

199 set nothing by: think nothing of.

200 halting: limping.

202 other gates: otherwise.

205 Sot: fool.

206 agone: ago.

207 set: dimmed by drink, closed.

208 passy measures pavin: (From Italian "passamezzo pavana") name of a dance, 可能意为 past all measures.

212—213 be dressed: have our wounds dressed.

215 gull: fool.

218 the brother of my blood: my own brother.

219 with wit and safety: having any sense of my own safety.

220 regard upon: look at.

Pardon me, sweet one, even for the vows
We made each other but so late ago.

DUKE. One face, one voice, one habit, and two persons,
A natural perspective, that is and is not!

SEBASTIAN. Antonio, O my dear Antonio!
How have the hours rack'd and tortured me,
Since I have lost thee!

ANTONIO. Sebastian are you?

SEBASTIAN. Fear'st thou that, Antonio?

ANTONIO. How have you made division of yourself?
An apple, cleft in two, is not more twin
Than these two creatures. Which is Sebastian?

OLIVIA. Most wonderful!

SEBASTIAN. Do I stand there? I never had a brother;
Nor can there be that deity in my nature,
Of here and every where. I had a sister,
Whom the blind waves and surges have devour'd.
Of charity, what kin are you to me?
What countryman? what name? what parentage?

VIOLA. Of Messaline: Sebastian was my father;
Such a Sebastian was my brother too,
So went he suited to his watery tomb:
If spirits can assume both form and suit,
You come to fright us.

SEBASTIAN. A spirit I am indeed;
But am in that dimension grossly clad
Which from the womb I did participate.
Were you a woman, as the rest goes even,
I should my tears let fall upon your cheek,
And say 'Thrice-welcome, drowned Viola!'

VIOLA. My father had a mole upon his brow.

SEBASTIAN. And so had mine.

VIOLA. And died that day when Viola from her birth
Had number'd thirteen years.

223 **each other**：to each other. **but**：only. **late**：recently.

224 **habit**：clothing.

225 **perspective**：幻境。 **that is and is not!**：是耶非耶，真假难分。

230 **Fear'st**：do you doubt.

232 **twin**：alike.

236 **deity**：magic power (of ubiquity，being in two or more places at once).

237 **Of**：of being.

239 **Of charity**：by charity，a phrase of exhortation，something like 'kindly tell me'.

243 **suited**：dressed.

247 **dimension**：bodily form. **grossly**：materially.

248 **participate**：share in common with others.

249 **goes even**：is in exact agreement.

SEBASTIAN. O, that record is lively in my soul!
He finished indeed his mortal act
That day that made my sister thirteen years.
VIOLA. If nothing lets to make us happy both
But this my masculine usurp'd attire,
Do not embrace me till each circumstance
Of place, time, fortune, do cohere and jump
That I am Viola: which to confirm,
I'll bring you to a captain in this town,
Where lie my maiden weeds; by whose gentle help
I was preserved to serve this noble count.
All the occurrence of my fortune since
Hath been between this lady and this lord.
SEBASTIAN. [*To* OLIVIA] So comes it, lady, you have been mistook:
But nature to her bias drew in that.
You would have been contracted to a maid;
Nor are you therein, by my life, deceived,
You are betroth'd both to a maid and man.
DUKE. Be not amazed; right noble is his blood.
If this be so, as yet the glass seems true,
I shall have share in this most happy wreck.
[*To* VIOLA] Boy, thou hast said to me a thousand times
Thou never shouldst love woman like to me.
VIOLA. And all those sayings will I over-swear;
And all those swearings keep as true in soul
As doth that orbèd continent the fire
That severs day from night.
DUKE. Give me thy hand;
And let me see thee in thy woman's weeds.
VIOLA. The captain that did bring me first on shore
Hath my maid's garments: he upon some action
Is now in durance, at Malvolio's suit,
A gentleman, and follower of my lady's.

256 **record**：recollection. **lively in my soul**：vivid in my memory.

257 **mortal**：human. **act**：activity.

259 **lets**：hinders.

260 **usurp'd**：assumed.

262 **cohere**：accord together. **jump**：agree，tally.

265 **weeds**：clothes. **whose**：that captain's.

269 **comes**：turns out.

270 **mistook**：mistaken.

271 **bias**：bent，preponderating tendency. **drew**：dragged.

272 **contracted**：married.

274 **maid and man**：virgin youth.

276 **glass**：指上面 225 行所说的 perspective.

277 **wreck**：shipwreck.

279 **shouldst**：would. **like to me**：as you would love me.

280 **over-swear**：swear over again.

282 **orbèd continent**：the sun. **continent**：后省略 keep.

287 **action**：legal process.

288 **durance**：confinement，imprisonment. **at Malvolio's suit**：at a suit with Malvolio.

OLIVIA. He shall enlarge him: fetch Malvolio hither:
And yet, alas, now I remember me,
They say, poor gentleman, he's much distract.

Re-enter CLOWN *with a letter, and* FABIAN.]

A most extracting frenzy of mine own
From my remembrance clearly banish'd his.
How does he, sirrah?

CLOWN. Truly, madam, he holds Belzebub at the stave's end as well as a man in his case may do: has here writ a letter to you; I should have given 't you to-day morning, but as a madman's epistles are no gospels, so it skills not much when they are delivered.

OLIVIA. Open 't and read it.

CLOWN. Look then to be well edified when the fool delivers the madman. [*Reads*] By the Lord, madam, —

OLIVIA. How now! art thou mad?

CLOWN. No, madam, I do but read madness: an your ladyship will have it as it ought to be, you must allow Vox.

OLIVIA. Prithee, read i' thy right wits.

CLOWN. So I do, madonna; but to read his right wits is to read thus: therefore perpend, my princess, and give ear.

OLIVIA. Read it you, sirrah. [*To* FABIAN.

FABIAN. By the Lord, madam, you wrong me and the world shall know it: though you have put me into darkness and given your drunken cousin rule over me, yet have I the benefit of my senses as well as your ladyship. I have your own letter that induced me to the semblance I put on; with the which I doubt not but to do myself much right, or you much shame. Think of me as you please. I leave my duty a little unthought of, and speak out of my injury.

THE MADLY-USED MALVOLIO.

290 **enlarge**：set at large，free.

291 **I remember me**：I recollect.

292 **distract**：distracted，mad.

293 **extracting**：distracting.

294 **his**：his frenzy.

296—297 **Belzebub**：the devil. **at the stave's end**：at bay.

297 **writ**：written.

300 **it skills not much**：it does not matter much.

302—303 **Look then**：pay attention then. **delivers**：speaks the words of.

305 **an**：if.

306—307 **allow Vox**：let people speak.

308 **Prithee**：I pray thee，please. **wits**：sense，judgement.

309 **madonna**〈意大利语〉：my lady.

310 **perpend**：consider.

318 **semblance**：outward appearance. **the which**：the letter.

OLIVIA. Did he write this?

CLOWN. Aye, madam.

DUKE. This savors not much of distraction.

OLIVIA. See him deliver'd, Fabian; bring him hither.

[*Exit* FABIAN.

My lord, so please you, these things further thought on,
To think me as well a sister as a wife,
One day shall crown the alliance on 't, so please you,
Here at my house and at my proper cost.

DUKE. Madam, I am most apt to embrace your offer.
[*To* VIOLA] Your master quits you; and for your service done him,
So much against the mettle of your sex,
So far beneath your soft and tender breeding,
And since you call'd me master for so long,
Here is my hand: you shall from this time be
Your master's mistress.

OLIVIA. A sister! you are she.

Re-enter FABIAN, *with* MALVOLIO.]

DUKE. Is this the madman?

OLIVIA. Aye, my lord, this same.
How now, Malvolio!

MALVOLIO. Madam, you have done me wrong,
Notorious wrong.

OLIVIA. Have I, Malvolio? no.

MALVOLIO. Lady, you have. Pray you, peruse that letter.
You must not now deny it is your hand:
Write from it, if you can, in hand or phrase;
Or say 'tis not your seal, not your invention:
You can say none of this: well, grant it then
And tell me, in the modesty of honor,
Why you have given me such clear lights of favor,
Bade me come smiling and cross-garter'd to you,

330 **One day**: the same day. **crown** (v.): bring to a successful conclusion.

331 **proper**: own.

332 **apt**: ready, willing. **embrace**: accept joyfully.

333 **quits**: sets free.

335 **mettle**: disposition, temperament.

349 **from it**: in a different way from it.

350 **invention**: composition.

353 **lights**: signals, indications.

To put on yellow stockings and to frown
Upon Sir Toby and the lighter people;
And, acting this in an obedient hope,
Why have you suffer'd me to be imprison'd,
Kept in a dark house, visited by the priest,
And made the most notorious geck and gull
That e'er invention play'd on? tell me why.

OLIVIA. Alas, Malvolio, this is not my writing,
Though, I confess, much like the character:
But out of question 'tis Maria's hand.
And now I do bethink me, it was she
First told me thou wast mad; then camest in smiling,
And in such forms which here were presupposed
Upon thee in the letter. Prithee, be content:
This practice hath most shrewdly pass'd upon thee;
But when we know the grounds and authors of it,
Thou shalt be both the plaintiff and the judge
Of thine own cause.

FABIAN. Good madam, hear me speak,
And let no quarrel nor no brawl to come
Taint the condition of this present hour,
Which I have wonder'd at. In hope it shall not,
Most freely I confess, myself and Toby
Set this device against Malvolio here,
Upon some stubborn and uncourteous parts
We had conceived against him: Maria writ
The letter at Sir Toby's great importance;
In recompense whereof he hath married her.
How with a sportful malice it was follow'd
May rather pluck on laughter than revenge;
If that the injuries be justly weigh'd
That have on both sides pass'd.

OLIVIA. Alas, poor fool, how have they baffled thee!

CLOWN. Why, 'some are born great, some achieve great-

356 **lighter**：less important.

357 **acting this**：when I acted in this manner.

358 **suffer'd**：allowed.

360 **geck and gull**：butt and dupe.

363 **character**：handwriting.

364 **out of question**：without question.

365 **bethink me**：remember.

366 **camest in**：you came in.

367 **presupposed**：enjoined beforehand.

369 **practice**：trick. **shrewdly**：cunningly. **pass'd upon**：played on.

370 **grounds**：motives.

375 **Taint**：前省略 to.

376 **wonder'd at**：regarded with surprise and joy.

376—380 此句可意译如下：In the hope that this may not happen，I most readily confess that it was myself and Toby who played this trick on Malvolio in view of his stubborn and unfriendly acts to which we took exception.

380 **writ**：wrote.

381 **importance**：importunity，solicitude.

384 **pluck on**：produce，excite.

385 **If that**：if.

386 **pass'd**：occurred.

387 **baffled**：treated shamefully.

ness, and some have greatness thrown upon them.' I was one, sir, in this interlude; one Sir Topas, sir; but that's all one. 'By the Lord, fool, I am not mad.' But do you remember? 'Madam, why laugh you at such a barren rascal? an you smile not, he's gagged:' and thus the whirligig of time brings in his revenges.

MALVOLIO. I'll be revenged on the whole pack of you.

[*Exit*.

OLIVIA. He hath been most notoriously abused.

DUKE. Pursue him, and entreat him to a peace:
He hath not told us of the captain yet:
When that is known, and golden time convents,
A solemn combination shall be made
Of our dear souls. Meantime, sweet sister,
We will not part from hence. Cesario, come;
For so you shall be, while you are a man;
But when in other habits you are seen,
Orsino's mistress and his fancy's queen.

[*Exeunt all, except* CLOWN.

CLOWN. [*Sings*]
When that I was and a little tiny boy,
  With hey, ho, the wind and the rain,
A foolish thing was but a toy,
  For the rain it raineth every day.

But when I came to man's estate,
  With hey, ho, &c.
'Gainst knaves and thieves men shut their gate,
  For the rain, &c.

But when I came, alas! to wive,
  With hey, ho, &c.
By swaggering could I never thrive,
  For the rain, &c.

390 I was one: I was one that had greatness thrust upon him (meaning he had been made to act as a parson). **interlude**: farce. **one Sir Topas**: Sir Topas is one of those who are born great.

391 that 's all one: that makes no difference. **'By the Lord, fool, I am not mad.'**: 此句学 Malvolio 在囚室向他求助时的哀告口气，见 IV. ii 101 行以下。

392—393 'Madam, ...': 此句学从前 Malvolio 在女主人前贬低 Feste (clown)时的口气。**an**: if. **gagged**: silenced.

394 whirligig: whipping top (used in a figurative sense, i. e., the wheel of history). 这里说 Malvolio 得到了报应。

399 convents: calls us together.

404 habits: clothes.

405 fancy's: love's.

406 歌六，见 177 页。

415 wive: get married.

But when I came unto my beds,
With hey, ho, &c.
With toss-pots still had drunken heads,
For the rain, &c.

A great while ago the world begun,
With hey, ho, &c.
But that's all one, our play is done,
And we'll strive to please you every day. [*Exit*.

421 **toss-pots**: topers，酒鬼。

ed your bed. Right next to your skin Trying to make contact Closer closer closer to

ly I had my wishes If I had my way I'd be all the time with you Each and every

ch I was a stocking Clinging to your thighs Everytime you move around I'd

r closer to you Closer got to get closer closer to you If I was a pair of boots I'd

ed Just being round your leg When I am dreaming Wishes & many wishes I'

side your lips Closer closer closer to you Closer got to get closer closer to you If

n your pocket When you feel the time was right I'd move when you want Wish I

ed your bed. Right next to your skin Trying to make contact Closer closer closer to